AF270813

Creating Safe Congregations:
Toward An Ethic of Right Relations

A Workbook for Unitarian Universalists

Edited by Patricia Hoertdoerfer and William Sinkford

Unitarian Universalist Association
Boston

This workbook is a project of the UUA Department for Congregational, District, and Extension Services and the Department of Religious Education, with Nancy Bowen, Betty Hoskins, Michelle Hunt, Fredric John Muir, Deborah Pope-Lance, Phyllis Rickter, and Gretchen Thomas.

Copyright © 1997 by the Unitarian Universalist Association, 25 Beacon Street, Boston, MA 02108. All rights reserved. Permission is granted to photocopy handouts and resources for use in this program only.

Printed in Canada.

ISBN 1-55896-349-9

05 04 03 / 9 8 7 6 5 4 3 2

Production Editor: Brenda Wong
Editorial Assistant: Debra Anderson
Text Designer: Suzanne Morgan
Cover Designer: Charlotte Burgess

Acknowledgments

Every effort has been made to trace the owner(s) of copyright material. We regret any omission and will, upon written notice, make the necessary correction(s) in subsequent printings.

Special thanks to the following for their contributions to the development of this workbook: Jade Angelica, Steve Howard, Beth Murray, and Tracey Robinson-Harris. In particular, we are grateful for the contributions of Fred and Betty Ward of the Unitarian Universalist Counseling and Education Service (Belle Mead, NJ) for their initial concepts and organization of the topics and resources for this workbook.

We acknowledge the use of the following material:

Introduction

Excerpts from "Making Love As a Means of Grace" by the Reverend Dr. Rebecca Parker are from *1992 Selected Essays, Unitarian Universalist Ministers Association.* (Boston: UUMA, 1992) Copyright © 1992 by the Unitarian Universalist Ministers Association. Reprinted by permission of the author.

Excerpts from the *Training Manual on Clergy Misconduct: Sexual Abuse in the Ministerial Relationship* by the Reverend Dr. Marie Fortune are reprinted by permission of The Center for the Prevention of Sexual and Domestic Violence.

An Ethic of Right Relations

Excerpts from *Getting to Yes* are adapted from *Getting to Yes*, second edition, by Roger Fisher, William Ury, and Bruce Patton. Copyright © 1981, 1991 by Roger Fisher and William Ury. Reprinted by permission of Houghton Mifflin Company. All rights reserved.

We Are All Responsible

Opening words by Kathleen McTigue are from *Singing The Living Tradition*, reading no. 706 (Boston: Beacon Press). Copyright © 1993 by the Unitarian Universalist Association. Reprinted by permission of the author.

Closing words by Sara Moores Campbell are from *Singing the Living Tradition*, reading no. 701 (Boston: Beacon Press). Copyright © 1993 by the Unitarian Universalist Association. Reprinted by permission of the author.

Excerpts from "Some Notes on the Ministry of the Clergy and the Laity" by James Luther Adams are from *Teamwork: Journal of the Universalist Ministers Association*, December 1957. Used by permission of the James Luther Adams Foundation.

Excerpts from "Finding Our Way: Responding to Clergy Sexual Misconduct" by Mary Moore, with Betty Hoskins, Mairi Maeks, and Phyllis Rickter are from *Transforming Thought Series, Volume III, 1992* (Boston: UU Women's Federation). Copyright © 1992 by Unitarian Universalist Women's Federation. Used by permission.

Excerpts from "Comforting the Bystanders and Cleansing the Religious Community" by Betty B. Hoskins and from "An Invitation to Readers" by Susann Pangerl are from *Edge of the Wave: Feminist Thought on Sexual Ethics*, edited by Susann Pangerl. Collegium Occasional Papers No. 3, 1993. Copyright © 1993 by Collegium: An Association of Liberal Religious Studies. Used by permission.

Excerpts from "Women Speak Out" by Phyllis Rickter are from the *World: A Journal of the Unitarian Universalist Association*, VII (1):27, January/February 1993. Reprinted by permission of the author.

The "Continuum of Abuse" by Dr. Bobbie Groth is adapted from the "Continuum of Family Violence" in *Village to Village* (Appendix I, p. 67), published by the Alaska Department of Public Safety. Reprinted by permission of the Alaska Department of Public Safety.

Abusing a Sacred Role

"Shared Ministry" by Robert Karnan is from *Awakened From the Forest* (Boston: Skinner House Books). Copyright © 1995 by the Unitarian Universalist Association. Reprinted by permission.

Acknowledgments continued on page 157.

Aiyanaha Rahman

Contents

Foreword

Ministry is the work and the reason of Unitarian Universalist congregations. Everything congregations do is ministry: the work of professional religious leaders; the work of lay leaders; the work of members. It is service to Unitarian Universalists, to civic communities, and to the world in perpetual hope that we will one day realize a world community with peace, liberty, and justice for all.

Are our congregations places of peace, liberty, and justice? Do justice, equity, and compassion govern their relationships? Too often our congregations have mirrored the alarming incivility of the secular culture. In a tradition that seeks active engagement with the struggles of the secular world, this is not surprising. It is, however, disappointing. For many Unitarian Universalists it is profoundly disturbing. Many of our congregations have become unsafe. All are at risk.

The culture of "talk radio" has entered our lives and our congregations. Conversations and discussions have taken on a level of heated rhetoric inappropriate for the gathered community of seekers. In this win-lose climate, attacking people rather than issues is an acceptable strategy. When members are attacked, diminished, dismissed, or discounted, the environment is unsafe. When the attack, dismissal, or discount occurs with good humor, smiles, and laughter, it is more unsafe because you can't see it coming. If it can happen to one member, it can happen to anyone, or to anyone foolish enough to take a position, offer another perspective, ask the difficult question, or accept a leadership role. If disrespectful, abusive, rude behavior is not confronted, it is understood to be condoned. If it is condoned it will be repeated. Who will be the next target? Would you feel safe? If so, why?

Our great, perhaps excessive, focus on our first Principle, the inherent worth and dignity of every person, has sometimes overshadowed our commitments to responsibility, justice, equity, compassion, and encouragement. Unitarian Universalists may think they must accept or endure bad behavior as an expression of their commitment to the inherent worth and dignity of every person. Not so. A respect for the inherent worth and dignity of every person should mean *every person*. We are not expected to accept behavior that diminishes another. We are called upon to address such behavior. When we discuss our children's physical and emotional safety, we are very clear about the lines of responsibility and accountability. We can be equally clear about the characteristics of healthy, respectful adult relationships.

Healthy, respectful adult relationships experience disagreements and conflicts. This is true of all relationships and especially true in our congregations where we have invited diversity of opinion and perspective. Disagreements and conflicts are inevitable in open, growing relationships. We might reasonably expect disagreement and welcome the breadth of perspective it offers us. Yet our congregations and their leaders are often afraid of disagreements. Recognizing the litigious tone and style of conflict in the popular media, fear may be a reasonable response, but it is not a helpful one. Congregation leaders are responsible for setting the standards for how we will express our disagreements. If a congregation cannot foster a welcoming place for the respectful expression of differences, it is not safe.

Leadership Response to Creating Safe Congregations

Our most powerful and effective tool in ministry is the act of naming. As leaders we must name the existing situation, acknowledge any disparity between our current reality and goals, and work to live our goals more nearly. While many aspects of creating a safe congregation can be done by small groups or committees, the overall stewardship of this initiative belongs at the highest level of leadership. This hard work may require courage to confront standards of silence. It may require patient tenacity in raising the issue again and again and again. It may require practice to learn new ways of interacting. It may require new levels of accountability. This hard work is the work of the congregation. It is ministry.

Regardless of where it originates, conversations between leaders and congregants of all ages need to be ongoing. By drawing the full congregation into conversation, it is possible to discover and name the congregation's existing behavioral norms. Such an investigation might try to answer some of these questions: How do we do things? How do we speak to one another? Are decisions based on an articulated, principled criteria? Are our primary lines of communications clear and public? What evidence can we find to support our respect for diversity of opinion? Do we confront and name rude, hurtful behavior? Do we have an implicit standard of consensus or unanimity?

Conversations about creating safe space can be a powerful community building experience, strengthening the congregation's understanding of itself, its goals and responsibilities. The very process we use to address these issues can begin to shape new standards of interaction among leaders and members of the congregation. Patient firmness will be needed because many will want to assert that there is no problem. The need to understand and provide safe space remains relevant without a present crisis.

We must teach and live our convenantal tradition of right relationships in our congregations. Our homes and congregations are the places where we can work to maintain the highest standards of safety and respectful relations.

Nancy Bowen
District Executive
Central Massachusetts and
Connecticut Valley

Introduction

The energy for creating this workbook came from dealing with cases of clergy sexual misconduct and child abuse in Unitarian Universalist congregations. For at least ten years, concerned groups and individuals have been working within the Association on these issues. Many congregations are trying to find justice, forgiveness, and health after experiencing misconduct and abuse within their community. Many congregational governing bodies, barraged with news reports of liability cases in other denominations, have invested time and energy in creating policies both to safeguard against incidents of abuse and to protect the congregation from legal action. Religious education leadership has been particularly responsive to issues of safety for children and youth.

This workbook addresses issues of safety and right relations in the congregational setting, between minister to congregation, congregant to congregant, adult to child, and child to child. The Unitarian Universalist Association believes it is a moral mandate to create and nurture these relations in the contexts of safety, integrity, and responsibility.

The assumptions that form the context of this workbook are three-fold. The first is the principle of "reverence for life." We affirm the worth of every person and the sacredness of every person's sexuality. In her essay "Making Love As a Means of Grace," the Reverend Dr. Rebecca Parker, president of Starr King School for the Ministry, writes, "A person's self-described positive sexual experiences disclose four sensibilities about our deepest being. The self we come to know in our best sexual encounters is, first, a self that is intimately connected with all of life. It is not a self-contained entity, but a center of feeling flooded by the whole world. Second, the self we come to know has the power to deeply affect another. It has the power of presence. It does not leave the world undisturbed but can activate profound pleasure in another by its very being. Third, the self we come to know takes joy in sheer being, in its own life and in the life it senses all around. Being itself is joyful, and being itself is a complex integration of breadth, created by receptivity to a vast field and intensity, created by the power to move another and to bring forth life. In sexual intimacy we can experience ourselves as having power—the power of receptivity and action combined, the power of feeling and doing, being moved and moving. We feel the force of our soul, the reality of our powerful presence in the world, and we feel it with joy."

Sexuality education and sexual ethics include intellectual, spiritual, social, emotional, behavioral, and interpersonal aspects as well as institutional concerns. They must attend to the evolutionary and unique challenges of development. We celebrate the bond of sexuality and spirituality, not as the focus of this workbook, but as something that can be explored in the religious education curriculum *About Your Sexuality* (AYS), and in the forthcoming lifespan religious education series *Our Whole Lives*.

The second assumption of this workbook is the pain of abuse, which contradicts our covenant as Unitarian Universalist congregations and our safety in Unitarian Universalist sanctuaries. In "Reflections Toward a Unitarian Universalist Theological Understanding of Clergy Sexual Abuse," an unpublished paper from the UUA Task Force on Congregational Response to Clergy Misconduct, the Reverend Thomas Mikelson, minister of First Parish in Cambridge, MA, writes, "In our congregations, we expect to be safe, not to have to be constantly on guard, as we have to be often in daily life, against the possibilities of exploitation and abuse. Spiritual growth leads persons back and forth between the faith community and the work outside, between risk and security, being tested and being nurtured. The rhythm of spiritual life is supported best by the sort of safety which is rarely found outside of religious community. Safety from abuse is one of the identifying signs of a healthy spiritual community. The fact that we gather in communities of faith suggests, beyond our hunger for spiritual growth, a need for the safety which allows us to let down defenses which usually stand in the way of self-examination. We can allow ourselves to be vulnerable only when we are reasonably confident that others in our communities will not take advantage of our vulnerability." (See UUA Resources, p. 115, for the full text of this paper.)

The third assumption is our definition of the Unitarian Universalist ministry as a "profession." Ministry and religious leadership provide services that require specialized knowledge and understanding. Power and authority are inherent in the ministerial role, which originates in the congregational covenant. Ministers are accountable to their religious communities by fiduciary responsibility.

As the Reverend Dr. Marie Fortune, founder and director of the Center for the Prevention of Sexual and Domestic Violence, states in her *Training Manual on Clergy Misconduct: Sexual Abuse in the Ministerial Relationship:* "A 'profession' is both (1) a calling and (2) an occupation requiring advanced education and training. 'Professional' quality work implies that the work meets or exceeds certain established standards. 'Professionals' are responsible for adhering to the standards of their profession, and are accountable to those whom they serve. The power and authority inherent in the role of minister is to be used in the interests of those served. . . . When ministers fail to carry out their fiduciary responsibility to those they serve, they betray a trust—the trust of their calling, the trust of the congregation, the trust of their colleagues and mentors."

Our congregations are responsible for being responsive and sensitive in open and honest ways to issues of abuse and violence. This workbook addresses these issues in terms of ethical relationships that form the foundation of our Unitarian Universalist Principles. Grappling with the spiritual and ethical dimensions of our faith can move us beyond abusive and dominator models of power to compassionate and empowering relationships.

This program can be used in a variety of settings and situations, such as adult education programs, congregational forums, RE teacher training workshops, and family and intergenerational programs. Its open-ended, workbook format invites you to supplement the program with historical and current resources important to your congregation.

Why Create a Workbook for Unitarian Universalist Congregations?

Our religious heritages—Unitarian, Universalist, and Unitarian Universalist—compel us to address the important, widespread, and complex social issues of sexual abuse and interpersonal violence. The subject of sexual abuse is complicated: Secrecy needs to be overcome; definitions need to be learned; ignorance needs to be dispelled; laws need to be understood; wounds need to be healed; rights and dignity need to be reestablished. Violence in interpersonal relationships, whether emotional, psychological, physical, or spiritual, profoundly affects all participants by diminishing human dignity and free choice.

In religious communities, breaches of trust and safety in congregations undermine the foundations of covenants, personally and communally. Unitarian Universalist congregations and the Unitarian Universalist Association of Congregations are committed to promoting justice for all people.

Unitarian Universalist Principles

This workbook is grounded in the Principles of our religious community, the Unitarian Universalist Association of Congregations.

❦ The inherent worth and dignity of every person

Every person's sexuality is sacred and worthy of respect; therefore, it is not to be violated.

❦ Justice, equity, and compassion in human relations

We treat others as we would want to be treated; therefore, sexual exploitation and interpersonal violence are wrong.

❦ Acceptance of one another and encouragement to spiritual growth in our congregations

Accepting each other as we are means doing no harm and fostering well-being in one's self and others.

❦ A free and responsible search for truth and meaning

In our relationship to others, our freedom of sexuality is as important as the responsibility for it.

❦ The right of conscience and the use of the democratic process within our congregations and in society at large

As a community and an institution, we are responsible for creating a secure, safe, and non-violent environment.

❦ The goal of a world community with peace, liberty, and justice for all

We have the opportunity to create the kind of environment that lends itself to peace, liberty, and justice in human interactions, and we can become a model for the rest of society.

❦ Respect for the interdependent web of all existence of which we are a part.

When we respect each person's sexual integrity, we honor the wholeness of life and respect the web of all existence.

Using This Program

Our primary goal is for participants and congregations to increase their understanding, skills, and resources in addressing and responding to the dehumanizing experience of interpersonal violence. This workbook will help Unitarian Universalists more readily identify unethical interpersonal conduct, gain better skills in making serious ethical choices, expand their understanding of core values in building right relations, and augment resources to enhance safety, integrity, and responsibility in sexual and social ethics. Materials provided with this program complement and enhance the resources of the UUA Departments of Ministry, Religious Education, and Congregational, District, and Extension Services; the twenty-three district offices; and various associate member and affiliate organizations. The authors and editors of this workbook encourage further work in congregations throughout the Association to discern right relations and appropriate actions in sexual and social ethics consistent with Unitarian Universalist values and principles.

Goals of the Program

- To help participants and congregations integrate values in this program into their system of values
- To help congregations maintain the integrity of ministerial relationships and Unitarian Universalist congregational relationships
- To help prepare congregations to protect vulnerable persons through effective education, responsible intervention, and appropriate responses
- To offer information and resources for leaders to provide opportunities for healing and justice for victims and congregations
- To provide educational resources for leaders to use in the development and implementation of congregational policies and procedures
- To offer information and resources for setting up prevention education programs
- To provide local, district, and Association partnership in recognition and celebration of a congregation's covenant for right relations and safe spaces.

Goals for Participants

Cognitive goals include:

- Becoming more aware of the issues of sexual abuse and interpersonal violence
- Learning the definitions of sexual harassment, abuse, and exploitation
- Developing an understanding of sexually abusive behaviors and chronically violent conduct
- Gaining an understanding of the issues of power and boundaries in abusive relationships
- Learning about positive exercises of interpersonal power and mutual respect in relationships
- Expanding knowledge about available resources.

Affective goals include:

- Probing participants' attitudes and feelings about sexual harassment and abuse
- Becoming more comfortable communicating feelings, values, and information about sexual abuse and unethical conduct with others
- Protecting, intervening, and responding appropriately to vulnerable people and/or victims.

Behavioral goals include:

- Exploring ways of preventing abusive situations
- Providing opportunities for support, justice, and healing
- Expressing and enjoying sexual and social ethics in responsible ways at each age of development.

How to Use This Workbook

Although this workbook offers a progression, it is not necessary to use it from front to back. It may be more meaningful to follow where the participants' needs and interests lead. Your congregation may choose a seven-session, four-session, or ten-session program. Here are some strategies to help you choose what to read and how to plan your schedule.

- Examine the seven sessions in the table of contents. These sessions address the following dimensions: clergy misconduct and abuse, peer harassment and abuse, and child abuse and neglect. Each of the sessions contains three elements: a process component that is a two-hour session plan where participants and congregations grapple with issues through reflection, exploration, and integration; a discussion essay that sets the issue and context for the theme; and resources included or referenced to facilitate the congregation's work. Each session can be used individually. All the discussion essays and resources needed for each session appear within that session.

- Examine the resources section at the end of the workbook. You may structure one or more sessions around some of the resources: the book *Is Nothing Sacred?* by Marie Fortune; the video *Not in My Church* by the Center for the Prevention of Sexual and Domestic Violence; a video and educational guide, *Reducing the Risk of Child Sexual Abuse in Your Church,* by Hammar, Klipowicz, and Cobble; and the book *Love Does No Harm: Sexual Ethics for the Rest of Us* by Marie Fortune.

- Read the first discussion essay, "An Ethic of Right Relations," in Session 1 for an overview of the core issues, dimensions, and contexts of this program. With this essay, work through the spiritual and ethical issues that have arisen in your congregation.

- Focus on an area of special concern in your congregation, such as justice making, healing the congregation, or prevention education programs.

Use this workbook as a motivator to gather people for education, moral discernment, spiritual nurturance, and ethical action. Together you can help focus reflection and action toward safe spaces and right relations in a transformative process.

Program Leaders

We strongly recommend experienced, skilled, non-judgmental co-leaders who can deal responsibly with emotional and sensitive material. Co-leadership provides significant benefits for both participants and leaders. Co-leaders can share the workload, provide feedback to one another, and reduce feelings of isolation. They also provide participants with more perspectives, experiences, leadership styles, and role models than an individual can provide.

Try to create a supportive, safe, comfortable, and respectful environment in which participants can risk feeling vulnerable and can experience and share at the levels where conviction and meaning grow. Leaders as well as participants need to be willing to re-examine their own attitudes and engage in discussions with careful thoughtfulness and integrity.

Leaders need to be familiar with the entire program and to be clear about their group's decision-making process to determine the number of sessions, the scheduling of sessions, and the timeframe for combining sessions in all-day or weekend retreats. Make a commitment to begin and end each session on time and ask participants for the same commitment. Such respectful use of everyone's time builds trust within the group.

Do the necessary preparation and planning. Having all materials and resources available before each session creates a relaxed and efficient environment. At the end of each session plan there is an evaluation and planning section. Your experiences and the quality of the program will be significantly enhanced if you take the time to evaluate experiences after each session and plan for the next one.

In planning your congregation's use of this workbook, acknowledge your religious community's strengths and gifts as well as its needs and shortcomings. Before beginning a process component or session plan, agree on guidelines for openness and sharing. Consider the following example and adapt, modify, or devise your own group guidelines.

Guidelines for Openness and Sharing

There is much potential for open sharing throughout this program. On many occasions you will invite participants to share what may be intimate material. Therefore, it is important that you let people know that you encourage them to speak only when they are comfortable, that it is always okay to pass if they choose not to share.

Establish a norm of respect for each other and each other's expression within the group. As much as possible, elicit the articulation and support of this norm from the participants. Engage people in discussing the value of respect in a group such as this and the destructive effects of sarcasm, 'put-downs,' and so on.

—from *In Our Hands: A Peace and Social Justice Program*

To make this program work, participants need to choose to be in relationship with each other for mutual growth and development and to want to become a congregation of right relations and safe spaces.

If this workbook helps you to move in new ways of thinking about right relations and safe space, into deeper spiritual convictions as Unitarian Universalists, and into more responsible non-violent ethical actions as a congregation, it has accomplished its goals. It is now in your hands.

1   An Ethic of Right Relations

Goals
- To explore right relations as an ethical guide to congregational life
- To gain an understanding of the complementary nature of an ethic of rules and an ethic of right relations
- To discover how an ethic of right relations changes how an ethical decision is understood or considered
- To practice using an ethic of right relations in making routine decisions in congregations.

Materials
- One copy of the discussion essay, "An Ethic of Right Relations," for each participant
- One copy of Resources 1, 2, 3, and 4 for each participant
- Each of the four features of an ethic of right relations printed on a piece of newsprint
- Copies of *Singing the Living Tradition*
- Chalice or candle and matches
- Newsprint, markers, and tape

Preparation
- Distribute the discussion essay to each participant with instructions to read it before the session begins.
- Read the discussion essay by Deborah Pope-Lance before the group meets.
- From the discussion essay, write on four pieces of newsprint each of the four features of an ethic of right relations.

Session Plan

Gathering and Centering   10 minutes

Light the chalice or candle and read responsively from reading no. 440, "From the Fragmented World," in *Singing the Living Tradition*.

Welcome participants by introducing yourselves. Invite the group to introduce themselves by name, how long they have been Unitarian Universalists, and how long they have been affiliated with or members of your congregation.

Give participants a brief overview of this workbook and its goals. Invite them to express what they hope to gain from this experience.

Focusing   10 minutes

Invite participants to discuss and agree upon the group's guidelines for openness and sharing. Say something like, "There is much potential for open sharing throughout this program. On many occasions we will invite participants to share what may be intimate material. Therefore, it is important that people speak only when they are comfortable; it is always okay to pass if people choose not to share. By establishing a norm of respect for each other and our expression within the group, we want to ensure safety and right relations for all participants."

Engage participants in discussing the value of respect and confidentiality in a group and the destructive effects of sarcasm and put-downs. Print your group's guidelines for openness and sharing on newsprint and post it as a reminder for each session.

Reflecting   10 minutes

Review the goals for this session with the group. Then focus the participants' attention on the discussion essay. Read these quotes on the theme "We Are All Related":

"Why should we not enjoy an original relation to the universe . . . " —Ralph Waldo Emerson

"In the beginning is relationship . . . is a freedom together . . . one must commit oneself to a conjunction with the other—but it is not selfless—it is a maintaining of the self in mystic balance and integrity—like a star balanced with another star."—Martin Buber, *I and Thou*

"Participation is a holy thing . . . that gives body and form to justice."—James Luther Adams

"Creative Interchange is a process in relationship in which individuals express themselves truly and fully to one another; in which each welcomes and seeks to understand the undisguised individuality of the other; each understands the view held by the other and absorbs (that understanding) into a personal view."—Henry Nelson Wieman, *Seeking a Faith for a New Age*

"In the different voice of women lies the truth of an ethic of care, the tie between relationship and responsibility. . . . While an ethic of justice proceeds from the promise of equality—that everyone should be treated the same—an ethic of care rests on the premise of non-violence—that no one should be hurt."—Carol Gilligan

"Everything is interconnected. All is relationship."—Starhawk

"Respect for the interdependent web of all existence of which we are a part."—Seventh Unitarian Universalist Principle

Ask participants to reflect silently for two minutes on these statements and then as a group to share reactions and comments to these statements.

Ask the following questions to elicit discussion:

- Is this an observation or a belief?
- What does this relatedness mean for you?
- How do you observe or not observe, believe or not believe in interdependence?

Exploring   75 minutes

Distribute and read each of the three ethical dilemmas from Resources 2, 3, and 4. Summarize Gilligan's observations that there are gender-related differences in ethical decision making.

Break into three or four small groups. Ask each group to pick one of the three dilemmas or to outline a situation of their own. If they pick their own situation, ask one of the participants to write notes so it can be referred to. While relevant situations are desirable, it may be helpful to avoid current or unresolved cases.

Distribute Resource 1 to each participant. Invite each group to answer the questions and to discuss the extent to which relationships with others determined their chosen decision and course of action.

After 30 minutes, come back to the large group. Have each small group report what situation they considered, how they decided what to do, and, citing the roles they chose, what course of action they proposed.

Integrating   10 minutes

Read out loud the last paragraph of the discussion essay. Invite participants to reflect in a moment of silence on the values each of them hopes more fully to express or exercise in their own relating.

Ask participants to share briefly their values, further actions, or insights gained from the experience of this session.

Closing   5 minutes

Gathering around the chalice or candle, invite participants to read in unison reading no. 501 from *Singing the Living Tradition*.

Evaluation and Planning

Consider the following questions. Reflect on them and discuss them with your co-leader(s).

1. How do I feel about this session now?
2. What was good and not so good about this session? Why?
3. If I were to lead this session again, what would I do differently?
4. What preparations do I need to make for the next session?

An Ethic of Right Relations
Deborah J. Pope-Lance

One the most difficult ethical moments I have experienced as a minister involved not a morally complicated public issue, but a routine situation—a meeting of the board of trustees. That night we were to consider the congregation's canvass and budget. Financially pinched, the board was inclined to cut and trim expenses. I suggested to them, "Before you cut every item, you may want to consider what items are religiously essential. Consider, for example, what items are necessary for the congregation to fulfill its religious purposes and principles in a basic minimum way."

They responded, "This isn't about religion. It's about being fair. If we are going to cut, we must cut everything the same. Cutting the budget is difficult enough without bringing in religion." Not to consider religion, especially in a religious context, struck me as ethically difficult, even morally suspicious.

Religion to some people is specific doctrines, traditions, or institutions, something that lives apart from the rest of life. But to many others, religion is the beliefs, meanings, and values by which one lives one's life. In this sense, religion has everything to do with how we understand anything and how we act. The congregation's budget and the way it is planned and raised is an expression of what the congregation and its leaders believe. The budget reveals religious values. My questions suggested that a religious budget *ought* to be an expression of religious belief. This "ought" is the link between religion and ethics.

Ethics is the consideration of how people ought to behave given what they believe and value. Religious values and meaning suggest some behaviors and not others, some decisions and not others. Ethics asks us to choose intentionally and to act with integrity on what we believe and value.

At this budget meeting, the actions of the congregational leadership expressed an important rule. If the budget had to be cut, it had to be fair and equitable. It is a good rule, even a right rule, accurately invoking the second Unitarian Universalist Principle—"justice, equity, and compassion in human relations." In citing this rule, the leaders did not consider other important beliefs and values. What about compassion, the belief that help ought to go to those whose need is greatest or who are most dependent or most vulnerable?

Rules are helpful in ethics. Expressive of important values, rules offer clear and accessible guidance, especially under stress or challenge. But an ethic of only rules is not adequate to the complicated situations we encounter in and out of our congregations. Nor is it adequate to express fully in our congregations or ourselves our values and beliefs. Another approach—an ethic of right relations—can balance an ethic of right rules and empower a fuller expression of intended beliefs and values.

By way of outlining an ethic of right relations, I will discuss three examples of routine dilemmas. Each one illustrates the ethical dimensions of a common congregational issue. Each also describes a routine conflict within the context of a congregational relationship—between a minister and congregants, among congregant groups, and between a congregation and the association of congregations.

I will describe each example as it is commonly understood and resolved and then outline how an ethic of right relations can alter how one understands and resolves these routine dilemmas.

Case 1. A young, single minister who has recently settled in a medium-sized congregation in a small city worries about how to date. "The rules," reminds one colleague, "certainly discourage, even prohibit, you from dating within the congregation." The minister protests, "Where is it written that I am supposed to give up having a personal life? Where is the rule that says I can't have a personal or intimate relationship with an adult who happens to be a member of my congregation? In this community who else is there?"

Rules prohibiting a minister from entering an intimate relationship with a congregant were intended to support a minister's capacity to serve members and friends of a congregation. The rule gives priority to professional rather than personal relationships. However, the rule does not reflect an appreciation of a small community's limitations. And the settlement of a young, single minister in a community where everyone is a member or friend of the parish does not reflect an appreciation of a single minister's basic needs. The connection between fulfilling a minister's basic personal needs and satisfying professional responsibilities has not been considered.

Rules can provide clear and accessible ethical guidelines. But they may not always serve good sense, good health, or their intended purpose. In this case, a minister's capacity to fulfill professional responsibilities may be adversely affected by a minister's best efforts to address basic personal needs. If a minister ignores the rule and dates within the congregation, he or she may reduce his or her capacity to serve as minister to some people or in some situations. If a minister ignores personal needs, he or she may use professional relationships to fulfill personal needs, thereby increasing the risk of harming individuals or abusing one's role. *Rules do not serve ethical decision making adequately or well if following them undermines the principle or value they were intended to serve.*

Case 2. Members and friends of a suburban congregation have spent two years talking about being a Welcoming Congregation. (A Welcoming Congregation is a congregation that has decided to be intentionally inclusive of gay, lesbian, bisexual, and transgender persons in all aspects of their religious community.) They considered how welcoming the congregation was or wanted to be and how to go about being intentionally welcoming.

Valuing an educational and democratic process, every member and friend had a chance to think the issue through and to explore their feelings before a vote was taken. At a congregation meeting, several people spoke of the religious principles involved in such a declaration. A few gave impassioned speeches on justice and civil rights; several others spoke of a belief in the inherent worth and dignity of all persons. No one spoke against the declaration itself. Some people expressed concern about having a vote on this sort of issue. Agreeing with those who had already spoken, they too considered it a matter of religious principle. "If you have this vote and make this declaration," they argued, "it will dictate belief for everyone in the congregation. People in this congregation have a right to believe anything they want." They argued that the congregation ought not to vote on anything that would infringe on this individual right.

Individual freedom of belief is fundamental to Unitarian Universalism. So universally acknowledged, this freedom operates as a clear rule within our congregations. There are Principles and Purposes, but acceptance of a specific creed is not required for membership. Rather, one must only find oneself in sympathy with the congregation. The principle that affirms "the inherent worth and dignity of all persons" is, in part, the religious basis for freedom of belief. Each person is respected as a valuable source of religious truth. But if the congregation does not vote because it does not wish to infringe on the freedoms and inherent worth of some people, it may risk infringing upon others' inherent dignity and worth. If the inherent worth and dignity of some people is compromised, how respected or safe is the inherent worth and dignity of anyone? Must protecting individual rights and freedoms mean compromising justice and compassion? How does the congregation's leadership know what to do?

A rule based on only one principle may conflict with another similarly valued principle. *Rules do not serve ethical decision making adequately or well if following them disregards one principle to uphold another.*

Case 3. A congregation objects to the Unitarian Universalist Association's requirement that it make a minimum financial contribution to receive unlimited Association services and staff support. Voting privileges may be limited as well if the congregation's Annual Program Fund contributions fall below a certain level. The congregation protests. "This rule interferes in a congregation's right to self-governance. We need to be able to decide how we will spend our resources. You can't make us contribute a certain amount; it violates congregational polity." Unless this requirement is withdrawn, the congregation may withdraw from the Association.

Congregational polity is fundamental to Unitarian Universalism. Intended to safeguard religious freedom, the right of local governance protects the congregation from dogmatic or authoritarian interference from outside sources such as kings or popes. Does congregational polity require the delivery of services for free? Should it require the Association to provide more services than it can fund from the support that members contribute? Why be a member of an association whose only reason for being is to serve its members if, as a member, you don't support it?

Rules that outline the extent of authorities and freedoms may be unrealistic and fail to meet the basic needs necessary to render those authorities and freedoms valuable and useful. *Rules do not serve ethical decision making adequately or well if following them undermines the values, persons, and organizations they were created to serve.*

Rules Serve Relationships

Ethical decision making based on rules is modeled on the Ten Commandments. Moses, with God's help, outlined a list of do's and don'ts to be learned and followed: Do not steal. Do not kill. Do not commit adultery. Strict adherence to these rules promised to bring people correct decisions and actions. But the Ten Commandments did not cover every circumstance or contingency. Rabbinical commentaries and extensive sections of scripture outline numerous exceptions to the strict adherence to these and other rules.

The basis for the Ten Commandments was a covenant that God made with Israel. Covenant is a religious term describing a relationship of commitment and responsibility. The covenant between Israel and God is described in the Book of Genesis: "I will be your God and you [Israel] will be my people." The Ten Commandments, indeed all the law and the prophets and the Hebrew scriptures, gave expression to this covenant.

A covenant is not a contract. It neither exacts obligations nor accords rights. A covenant is not a creed. It does not dictate correct doctrine or belief. A covenant outlines a relationship and is a voluntary and unconditional agreement between one or more people. In their covenant with God, people promised to act in ways that express, value, and serve the relationship. Rules developed to guide these promises. The test of any rule, nonetheless, was how well it served the relationship between God and humanity.

At times throughout Jewish and Christian history, believers and leaders have followed or enforced rules in an obsessive and exacting manner. Rules became detached from the relationships they were intended to express and serve. For example, the early puritan churches were often exactingly narrow in enforcing religious rules. For many years, the Reverend Israel Loring, minister of First Parish in Sudbury, Massachusetts from 1704-1771, would not christen babies born on Sunday. Loring believed that babies were born on the same day of the week as they were conceived. Since Sunday was the sabbath and by the commandments to be kept as a day of prayer and devotion to God, a child born on that day gave evidence of his or her parent's non-adherence to the law. Loring was guided by this rule absolutely until one Sunday morning his wife delivered twins. Thereafter, he reportedly christened all Sunday born babies retroactively, beginning no doubt with his own.

The story may be apocryphal but it illustrates well the risks of following rules without regard to the relationships they were intended to serve. The early Puritans knew that they were utterly dependent for survival upon God and one another. The rules, if somewhat quaintly ignorant, were intended to safeguard these relationships. A baby and his or her parents needed to be properly connected to God by prayer and worship, but if following the rule did not serve to keep the covenanted congregant members connected and safe, then it logically followed that the rule needed to be modified or reconsidered.

Humanity's religious development can be illustrated as a balance between a rule-based ethic and a relationship-based ethic. When the fulcrum falls too far to one side, the other is reasserted for balance. The emphasis on love and belief in the teachings of Jesus has been understood as a re-balancing response to an exacting attention to the law and the commandments. And the Protestant Reformation has been understood as a correcting rebellion against the capricious sale of indulgences and pardons by church authorities.

Rules are one method by which relationships are valued. *But the test of any rule's ethical capacity is how well it expresses, values, serves, and protects the relationship that generated the rule.*

An ethic of right relations will not replace an ethic of right rules, but it provides a corrective test of the capacity of any rule. Ultimately it will make it more likely that the truths we acknowledge and the values we cherish will be expressed in our lives and our world.

Valuing Relationships

The practical significance of an ethic of right relations is graphically demonstrated by the work of Carol Gilligan. Gilligan studied ethical decision making among adolescents and observed a distinctly different response in boys and girls. Boys more consistently described the ethical dilemma Gilligan posed as a conflict between the values of property and life. Boys based their suggested action on what they considered to be the "right thing to do." In contrast, girls more frequently saw the same ethical dilemma not as a "math problem with humans," but as "a narrative of relationships." Girls based their suggestions for action on the value and quality of relationships and on "an awareness of connection between people" and on "the need for response."

Gilligan's identification of gender differences in moral development has profoundly affected the study of ethics and ethical decision making. Her work has encouraged the fuller participation of women and women's perspectives in moral debate. But her most significant contribution has been to utterly alter the conversation. What once was a conversation that considered the relative merits of rights and rules must now consider the value of relationships. Valuing relationships will enlarge the number of choices and change the understanding of responsibility. Consider how valuing relationships alters decision making in the three cases cited earlier.

Case 1. How will valuing relationships change the single minister's ethical concerns? Beyond wondering and worrying about rules for dating, the minister would have been better served by considering the various relationships that generated the rules. Instead of viewing personal and professional needs as being in opposition, the minister could have considered how personal and professional needs and responsibilities are related. Previously unimagined choices would have appeared. In particular, the minister could have asked, How do I satisfy my personal needs in a way that supports the fulfillment of my professional obligations? The minister might have observed that as a single person who is without immediate family ties, he or she might choose settlements where there is a greater opportunity to attend to personal interests and needs outside professional contexts. Or in considering limited professional opportunities, this minister might consider arrangements for time away from the professional context to attend to personal needs.

A congregation wanting to choose this minister needs to ask questions about the connection between personal and professional needs and obligations. A minister and an isolated congregation considering a settlement together will be well served to consider how the minister's basic personal needs will be met so that professional responsibilities may be fulfilled. Without a shared consideration of the potential conflict between personal and professional issues, the risk of misconduct or ill health increases.

Case 2. How will valuing relationships alter the conversation about inherent worth and individual rights? If the congregation's leadership considers the valuable connection between an individual and the congregation, they will understand the dilemma not as a competition for the exercise of rights, but as a challenge to affirm shared rights.

The congregational vote asks the whole congregation to affirm the inherent dignity and worth of all people by making intentional efforts to affirm the inherent dignity and worth of a specific group of persons who have experienced disaffirmation. While justice and fairness continue to be important ethical standards, so too will be how the congregation extends care and compassion. If the leadership considers the value of connection among all members, they will value the connecting and relating involved in pre-vote discussions and understand that it is as essential to the decision as the vote itself. In this way, they might ask themselves, How do we as a congregation continue to stay in conversation about these issues? How might we see this vote, not as a win/lose situation where losers leave, but as part of a commitment to stay in relationship and conversation about a shared solution?

Case 3. How will valuing relationships change a congregation's concern that requirements, financial or otherwise, by the Association inappropriately interfere with local governance? Local congregations are members of the Association for a reason—to receive help with educational curricula, to use job placement services, to enjoy wider recognition by use of its name or publicity.

If the congregation's leadership had considered what needs they hoped to have satisfied or what causes they hoped to further in a relationship with the Association, they might have concluded it prudent to provide appropriate financial support. Without the individual congregation's support, the Association would be ineffective in meeting the congregation's needs and may cease to further the cause that created the relationship.

If the congregation and association leadership considered what was wanted or expected from the relationship, they would see the financial support issue not as a competition of needs or as a conflict for control, but as a conversation leading to the fulfillment of shared goals. In this conversation, the leadership will discover not the limits of its obligations, but the extent of its capacity to achieve these shared goals.

Four Features of an Ethic of Right Relations

By valuing relationships, an ethic of right relations changes ethical conversation and decision making. The following features suggest some guidelines for encouraging this change and exercising an ethic of right relations.

1. An ethic of right relations considers relationships when making ethical decisions.

Interdependence is affirmed in the seventh Unitarian Universalist Principle: "We, the member congregations of the Unitarian Universalist Association, covenant to affirm and promote . . . Respect for the interdependent web of all existence of which we are a part." Starhawk, a neo-pagan religionist, expresses this principle when she echoes the Native American affirmation, "We are all related." She reminds us that, "Everything is interconnected. All is relationship." An ethic of right relations asks that the interdependent relationship of all things guides how people act and choose, how people relate with all things.

An affirmation of interdependence and the value of relationships is not new. Jewish theologian Martin Buber called attention to the essential relationship between God and humanity. "In the beginning is the relation," wrote Buber in *I and Thou*. This essential covenantal relationship provides guidance on how people ought to relate to one another—in a way that reflects and expresses God's committed connection with humanity, or what Buber called "I/Thou."

An ethic of right relations is the moral implication of interdependence. It asks that relationships be considered prominently in ethical decision making. Relationships should be accorded value in the same way that rights and privileges, rules and principles have been accorded value in ethical decision making. The impact of moral decisions on the quality and health of a relationship should be given serious attention in weighing choices. If a specific action may violate a right or a rule, how well it upholds the value of relationship should also be assessed. A test, then, of any action under an ethic of right relations is whether it shows evidence of having considered and valued relationships and connections.

A recent industrial catastrophe provides a sterling example of decision making informed by an ethic of right relations. The Malden Mills, a major textile manufacturer in Massachusetts, experienced a devastating fire just prior to the 1995 winter holidays. Much of the company's buildings were destroyed or left unusable. Thousands of people were left without work. Common business practice is guided by a rule that if a company has an interruption in work demand, regardless of cause, people are laid off until there is work. The practice of furloughing unnecessary workers—even if temporarily—is considered prudent management because it abides by this rule. The owner of Malden Mills would have been acting in an ethically reasonable and fair manner if he furloughed the mill workers indefinitely. Instead, the mill owner considered relationships. He recognized the connection and interdependence between the workers and the company, between the company and its workers and the community, and between the workers and their families. He recognized that many workers had been with the textile manufacturer for years, some even for generations; that most had no other means of support, nor did the community businesses whose clientele were mill workers. The mill owner also recognized that the mills, when rebuilt, would need the experienced workers back at work. Valuing and considering these relationships, the mill owner decided to pay the mill workers until they were back at work.

2. An ethic of right relations encourages relating and connecting in decision making or problem solving.

Because relationships are valued, they should be preferred and encouraged. For example, membership in an association of congregations is itself an assertion that a shared, common life offers something of value that individual life cannot. Similarly, membership in a congregation is an affirmation of the rewards of a shared religious journey. "Participation," theologian James Luther Adams observed, is a "holy thing . . . that gives body and form to justice."

In this way, an ethic of right relations values relating as a means of decision making and problem solving. Where an ethic based on rules and principles alone might use arbitration and negotiation as a method of resolving problems or decisions, an ethic of right relations suggests that this type of conflict resolution may not encourage connection or meet anyone's needs. A commitment to connecting and relating, however, brings an opportunity for greater understanding and learning and the possibility of discovering otherwise unimaginable solutions.

Roger Fisher and William Ury, authors of *Getting to Yes*, tell a story in which relating as a means of resolution leads to greater understanding and a mutually satisfying, previously unimaginable solution. Two girls need the only orange available for a recipe each is preparing. "I must have it," said one, "or I cannot make the orange nut muffins." "But if you use it," says the other, "I won't be able to prepare the glaze for my chicken recipe." The girls imagine no other way to settle their conflict fairly and so split the orange in half. One scrapes the peel of her half adding it to the muffins. The other squeezes the juice from her half and makes the glaze. Had they been committed to relating and gaining greater understanding of each other, rather than merely arbitrating their equal claims, they would have discovered a resolution satisfying to both—giving the whole of the peel to one and all of the juice to the other.

Henry Nelson Wieman, a liberal Protestant theologian, understood God and all that was holy and of ultimate value as immanent and present in human relating. Like Buber and Adams, Wieman understood God's immanence in human relating to provide a model for how humans ought to relate to one another. In *Seeking Faith for a New Age: Essays on the Interdependence of Religion, Science and Philosophy*, he called this model "creative interchange: . . . a process in relationship in which individuals express themselves truly and fully to one another; in which each welcomes and seeks to understand the undisguised individuality of the other; each understands the view held by the other and absorbs (that understanding) into a personal view. In this way, each expands and enriches the fullness of experience and increases the depth of reality which enters into personal consciousness." Such a relationship brings into being an enlarging truth and, writes Wieman, like the power many have called divine, "can transform us like nothing else can."

Under an ethic of right relations, respecting others and resolving conflicts may suggest the use of fairness and justice. But it also suggests that respecting others and resolving conflicts may mean relating, despite the conflict, in a commitment to stay connected, to learn together, and to discover mutually satisfying resolutions that could not be discovered or imagined alone.

3. An ethic of right relations understands relationships as expressions of value, commitment, purpose, and covenant.

One reason relationships are valued is because they are expressions of promises, commitments, covenants, and purposes. Similar to God's covenant with Israel, many relationships are everyday covenants, voluntary agreements between people who promise to act in ways that express and serve the valued relationship and its intended promise and purpose.

One common covenantal relationship, for example, is that between parent and child. A parent-child relationship is intended initially to serve the growing needs of a child. Although it may be satisfying to either or both, if a parent-child relationship fails to meet the basic needs of a child, it will not have fulfilled its intended purpose. Admittedly, a relationship between a parent and child is one of inequality and dependence. But the purpose and the promise is shared: the child's to grow, the parent's to foster growth in the child. As every parent knows, decisions arise that appear to place the child and the parent's interests at odds. An ethic of right relations would look for help in such decisions by asking: What is the shared purpose or promise intended or expressed in this relationship? How will this decision or action express or serve this purpose or promise?

Other common covenantal relationships are characterized by interdependence and equality. Committed couples, for example, are equal and mutually dependent partners. Congregations are members of equal status and privilege within an association of congregations. Both partners and congregations have different resources, however, and may take on distinctly different commitments or tasks. These differences may create activities where they are not equal in capacity or responsibility.

In relationships, people may have different capacities. A parent has mature abilities; a child is developing. People may have different roles. In a ministerial relationship, a minister's role is to address the spiritual needs of a congregant. These differences may change the power each may exercise in the relationship, but they do not change the fact that the relationship is an expression of a shared value, commitment, purpose, or covenant.

An ethic of right relations leads one to ask what shared interests or values are expressed in this relationship. How well will these shared interests or values be fulfilled or fostered by the proposed decision or action? A decision or action that serves only one or the other in a relationship while adversely affecting the shared relationship or its intended values, will not reflect a valuing of relationships or foster the relationship's expression of value, commitment, or purpose. An ethic of right relations responds to a diversity of interests in a way that presumes not conflict but relationships of shared purpose and value. In this sense, diversity is not a problem to be solved or controlled but a resource toward a solution.

Process theologian Bernard Loomer makes an important contribution to an understanding of right relations. In his article, "Two Conceptions of Power" in the spring 1976 issue of *Process Studies Special Issue: Essays in Honor of Charles Hartshorne,* he describes "unilateral power" and "relational power." Unilateral power is "the capacity to produce an effect or to influence another," to control or manage another. Relational power is "the capacity to be influenced or to sustain a relationship" by or with another. Unilateral power assumes that one actor directs, manages, or coerces another into the actor's desired action. Relational power generates mutually determined action. Unilateral power has an inherent potential for abuse or violence because by it one person is controlled and molded to another's whim. Relational power is inherently inclusive and mutual because by it everyone is created and action is determined. In relational power everything is a consequence of relationships with others. "The commitment, within relational power," Loomer notes, is not to the self only and "not to each other but to the relationship which is creative of both."

The test of any behavior or decision under this feature of an ethic of right relations is how well it serves to fulfill, foster, and further the relationship's promise, commitment, purpose, or value. In an ethic of right relations one asks: What are the promises and commitments intended by this relationship? How consistent is this decision or behavior with these? Will this decision or behavior increase or decrease the capacity to fulfill the purposes of the relationship? Will it further them or put them at risk? Will this decision or behavior make it more rather than less possible to fulfill commitments, and in effect, to be more of who and what we aspire to be at our best, together?

4. An ethic of right relations encourages the exercise of values in relating. Relationships are valuable in part because they are the arena in which everything happens. Relating is how values are exercised—how care is extended, justice assured, love shared, and anger addressed. Relating is how we act and respond, react and re-respond.

Carter Heyward, Episcopal priest and feminist theologian, uses the phrase "right relations" to speak of just relationships and to call for justice making. "Evil is the violation of relation in human life," writes Heyward. The power in relation inherent in human life is what, according to Heyward, we may claim to change the world. Relation is how justice is made and re-made. Redressing wronged relations and confronting those power and principalities that violate relations and harm human well-being make for justice.

Justice making, in western religious traditions, has involved identifying those who are responsible, holding them accountable for their actions, and compelling them to make amends for injury they have caused. Responsibility is attributed to persons who intended, caused, or could have prevented adverse consequences. Legal liability is similarly determined. The law says a person is liable for any damages resulting from circumstances one could have or should have controlled.

An ethic of right relations calls for something more. An ethic of right relations calls us to be responsible not only in the past to our values and beliefs, in this case justice and fairness, but also in the present. We may not be responsible for what happened in the past, but we are responsible for how we respond and for what happens now.

Consider this example: How should we respond to people who have been victimized, especially if they have been victimized by those whose responsibility was to serve and care for them, such as ministers or teachers? Under an ethic of right relations, we should hold those who victimized them accountable *and* we should support them in healing. But does this mean we should provide them with financial support? Legal counsel often advises against financial support because it may be seen as an admission of guilt, that is, as an admission that we could have or should have done something to prevent the victimization. An ethic of right relations encourages us to do what we can, here and now. Whether we were or could be considered responsible for what happened, we can be responsible for what happens now. What values do we seek to encourage and exercise in our relating? Do we value mercy? Then we may choose to be with and care for those who suffer. Do we value compassion? Then we may choose to support financially the healing of those who have been wronged and injured.

In this way an ethic of right relations asks: What are the values and beliefs we affirm and want expressed in our relating *now*? An ethic of right relations acknowledges that disconnection and estrangement, conflict and breakdown, disappointment and hurt, happen in relating. Relating is how we change, forgive, learn, heal, and grow. Relating is not only how everything happens. Relating is how anything ever will happen. An ethic of right relations asks what can we do now.

Conclusion

An ethic of right relations alters the way we understand and consider ethical decisions. Ethical choices are served by rules and principles but need as well the enlarging view and balancing perspective of an ethic that values relationships. Utilizing an ethic of right relations, we and our congregations will be better equipped to meet complicated ethical challenges in and out of our congregations and to live our values and beliefs.

Features in an Ethic of Right Relations

Four features to consider:

- What relationships are affected by a decision?
- How could relating contribute to decision making?
- What are the shared values or purposes intended in affected relationships? for other relationships?
- What are the important values that need to be exercised in relating or responding to this situation?

Case Study   Describe one of the three situations discussed in Deborah Pope-Lance's essay.

Course of Action

If your group were a congregation's leadership, how might you proceed?

How might you proceed if you were a religious professional in this situation?

How might you proceed if you were an Association representative?

Values Expressed and Exercised in Relationships

Name the values.

How are these lived and learned?

Settlement of a Minister: An Ethical Dilemma

A young, single minister, who has recently settled in a medium-size congregation in a small city, wonders and worries about how to date. "The rules," reminds one colleague, "certainly discourage, even prohibit, you from dating within the congregation."

The minister protests, "Where is it written that I am supposed to give up having a personal life? Where is the rule that says I can't have a personal or intimate relationship with an adult who happens to be a member of my congregation? In this community who else is there?"

Rules prohibiting a minister from entering an intimate relationship with a congregant were intended to support a minister's capacity to serve members and friends of a congregation. The rule gives priority to a professional rather than a personal relationship. However, the rule does not reflect an appreciation of a small community's limitations. Neither does the settlement of a young, single minister in a community where everyone is a member or friend of the parish reflect an appreciation of a single minister's basic needs. Nor does it consider the connection between fulfilling a minister's basic personal needs and satisfying professional responsibilities.

- What are the issues for a congregation facing the possibilities of calling a young, single minister?

- What are the responsibilities of the search committee? of the members? of the ministerial settlement representative? of the UUA Ministry Department Settlement Office?

- Is there a leadership role for the UUMA chapter? district churches?

- What are the effects for a congregation facing this possibility? for a minister facing this possibility?

The Welcoming Congregation: An Ethical Dilemma

The members and friends of a suburban congregation have spent two years discussing what it might mean for them to be a Welcoming Congregation. (A Welcoming Congregation is a congregation that has decided to be intentionally inclusive of gay, lesbian, bisexual, and transgender persons in all aspects of their religious community.) They had considered how welcoming the congregation was or wanted to be, and how to go about being intentionally welcoming.

Valuing the educational and democratic process, every member and friend had a chance to think the issue through and to explore their feelings before a vote was taken. At a congregation meeting several people spoke of the religious principles involved in such a declaration. A few gave impassioned speeches on justice and civil rights; several others spoke of a belief in the inherent worth and dignity of all persons. No one spoke against a declaration itself. Some people expressed concern about having to vote on this sort of issue. Agreeing with those who had already spoken, they too considered it a matter of religious principle. "If you have this vote and make this declaration," they argued, "it will dictate belief for everyone in the congregation. People in this congregation have a right to believe anything they want." They argued that the congregation ought not to vote in anything that would infringe upon this individual right.

- Individual freedom of belief is fundamental to Unitarian Universalism. What other issues is this congregation facing in the context of this dilemma?

- If the inherent worth and dignity of some is compromised, how respected or safe is the inherent worth and dignity of anyone? By protecting individual rights and freedoms, do you compromise justice and compassion?

- What are some possible responses available to congregational leaders facing this issue?

- How is the leadership to know what to do? Should they have the vote or not? What are possible consequences of a vote for the congregation?

Congregational Polity: An Ethical Dilemma

The Unitarian Universalist Association is an association of churches in which member congregations make financial contributions to support programs that are in turn made available to the members. In her essay, "An Ethic of Right Relations," Deborah J. Pope-Lance describes "A congregation (who) objects to the Association's requirement that they make a minimum financial contribution in order to receive the Association's services and staff support" by a decision to cease support of the Association. This is extreme and would presumably require careful consideration. Yet it is, of course, one alternative. After all, as Pope-Lance concludes: "The rule of congregational polity is fundamental to the liberal church."

- What are the issues for a congregation facing this possibility?

- What are the leadership responsibilities in a congregation considering this alternative? to the members? to the district? to the UUA?

- What other responses are available to congregational leaders facing this issue?

- Is there a leadership role for a cluster? the district? a neighboring congregation? an area UUMA chapter?

- What are the effects for a congregation facing this possibility?

2 We Are All Responsible

Goals
- To explore the legal, moral and ethical, and organizational dimensions of Unitarian Universalist leadership
- To explore issues of power and authority in Unitarian Universalist leadership
- To identify and define ways to build and sustain models of safe congregations and right relationship.

Materials
- One copy of the discussion essay for each participant
- Your congregation's mission statement, covenant, constitution, and bylaws
- One copy of Resource 5 for each participant
- Copies of *Singing the Living Tradition*
- Chalice or candle and matches
- Newsprint, markers, and tape

Preparation
- Distribute the discussion essay to each participant with instructions to read it before the session begins.
- Read the discussion essay by Betty Hoskins and Phyllis Rickter before the group meets.
- Review the cases of misconduct and abuse in Resource 5.
- Familiarize yourself with Bobbie Groth's diagram in Resource 5.

Session Plan

Gathering and Centering   5 minutes

Light the chalice or candle and read these opening words:

> May the light around us guide our footsteps,
> and hold us fast to the best and most righteous that we seek.
> May the darkness around us nurture our dreams,
> and give us rest so that we may give ourselves to the work of the
>   world.
> Let us seek to remember the wholeness of our lives

the weaving of light and shadow in this great and astonishing dance in which we move.

—Kathleen McTigue

Focusing 10-15 minutes

Ask the participants to introduce themselves and to share one critical characteristic of leadership. Invite them to explain briefly why this one element is vital to Unitarian Universalist leadership. Summarize the elements of leadership shared and review the goals for this session.

If this is the first gathering of this group for Creating Safe Congregations work, establish group guidelines. Refer to page 10 for the procedure.

Reflecting 10 minutes

In their essay, Betty Hoskins and Phyllis Rickter refer to effective Unitarian Universalist congregational leadership that "finds time to think through questions of authority, power, and truth-telling; has open discussion among minister, staff, and laypeople; knows when to ask for help and information; and knows it does not have all the answers."

Invite participants to reflect on these words and to share their comments and examples of effective congregational leadership from their experience and knowledge. Ask:

- What are the channels of authority and communication in your congregation?
- Are there open discussions on policy matters between professional and lay leadership?
- How do you access support, information, and resources?

Exploring 70 minutes

Adapt this activity to fit the size of your group.

- For a large group of eight or more, ask the group to review all five situations in Resource 5 and to respond to all the discussion questions.
- For small groups of three to four, ask participants to review, choose, and discuss one of the situations in Resource 5—clergy sexual misconduct and abuse, child neglect and abuse, peer harassment and abuse, congregational polity, or anti-racism. Each of the small groups needs a person to be a recorder and to take notes on a piece of newsprint.

Let the groups engage in discussion for 40 minutes.

Return to one group and either summarize pertinent leadership responses or invite summaries from the group recorders.

Integrating   15 minutes

Using your congregation's mission statement, constitution and bylaws, and policies and procedures documents, identify and define your congregation's next steps. Record responses on newsprint.

Engage the participants in a discussion of Bobbie Groth's diagram from Resource 5. Try to draw this continuum as a circle.

Invite responses. Ask, "What parts of the circle can be considered in congregational life? When are leadership, laypeople, staff, and clergy involved?"

Closing   5 minutes

Gather around the chalice or candle. Invite participants into a moment of silence.

Share these closing words by Sara Moores Campbell: "We receive fragments of holiness, glimpses of eternity, brief moments of insight. Let us gather them up for the precious gifts that they are and, renewed by their grace, move boldly into the unknown."

Sing "Spirit of Life" (hymn no. 123) or "Gathered Here" (hymn no. 389).

Evaluation and Planning

Consider the following questions. Reflect on them and discuss them with your co-leader(s).

1. How do I feel about this session now?
2. What was good or not so good about this session? Why?
3. If I were to lead this session again, what would I do differently?
4. What preparations do I need to make for the next session?

A Working Paper on Leadership
Betty Hoskins and Phyllis Rickter

> Is it not correct for us to say that one of the best ways to test a church is by the quality and participation of its laity? Our Universalist-Unitarian heritage from the beginning has been committed to "radical laicism. . . ."
>
> The priesthood of all believers in the tradition of radical laicism implied that every member of the church has the obligation to share in the work of reconciliation and healing which belongs to the mission of the church; it implied also that every member of the church has the privilege and obligation of participating in the shaping of the policies of the church. . . .
>
> The prophethood of all believers implied that every member of the church must share with the clergy the obligation of directing prophetic criticism at both the church and the society.
>
> —James Luther Adams,
> "Some Notes on the Ministry of
> the Clergy and the Laity," *Teamwork*

Who Is the Church Leadership?

We are all church leaders. It's part of belonging. Probably your experiences parallel ours: We volunteered and we were nominated. We became more and more involved. We decided to serve on a committee as a way to feel more like a part of the group. We find it's our turn to give back to the community. Soon, it's our turn to chair the committee. Then we're asked to serve on the board of trustees. Or the committee on ministry. Or the finance committee. Or the district board. Or a committee of the Unitarian Universalist Association. If we have children in the church school or we have teaching credentials, we're invited to work in the children's religious education or asked to join in planning the adult education program. Next we have a part in evaluating volunteers.

If we have expertise or interest in repairs or gardening, we'll find ourselves on the building and grounds committee; we may have to evaluate whether the building is a safe place—for the daily preschool, for the musician/organist practicing alone at night, for the minister counseling a troubled person. Whatever the size of the congregation, the same issues occur everywhere.

While inclusion in the church leadership may seem casual and informal, the responsibilities are not slight. The church board is ultimately responsible—not only for financial matters, but also for setting policy in many areas of church life. The board is obliged to ensure its policies are carried out. Issues of safety and of possible liability belong to the board. It also is ultimately responsible for the conduct of people who serve the church in official capacities. These include parish minister(s), the minister or director of religious education, music staff, perhaps a community minister, administrators, office staff, and custodial staff.

As Unitarian Universalists, we assume that board and committee members care about their religious community and want to reduce risks to its well-being. We assume that being Unitarian Universalists, they will ask many questions—ethical, legal, spiritual, practical, theological. They will look at problems from many different angles. They will try to handle difficulties with grace and fairness. That's why we stay committed to Unitarian Universalism.

What Is Effective Church Leadership?

Every church leader wants to be effective; knowing how to be effective is a more complex matter. We bring work styles with us and we learn new modes. We bring a variety of skills into the church setting. Some of us bring the analytical skills of science and the high-tech industry, the metaphorical skills of the humanities, business acumen and management skills, financial training, and the procedures of non-profit agencies. Still others bring legal training and knowledge of question-asking, evidence-gathering, and position-taking. Some of us bring professional codes as therapists, social workers, professors, nurses, health care providers, substance abuse counselors, and physicians. Others bring experience as loyal employees or consultants held accountable. Many of us have experience in community organizations staffed by volunteers.

This mixture of skills brings richness—but also complexity—to our leadership. In particular, the ethical, religious/spiritual/theological aspirations and the rule-based legal approaches appear to be on different wavelengths. Thus, effective leadership calls for multiple forms of reflection, diagnosis of many different kinds of situations, and thoughtful agreements about appropriate action.

What are appropriate methods? Frequently, we use our tried-and-true procedures and habits. When we're puzzled by others' behaviors, perhaps they are automatically drawing on models that worked elsewhere, in business or volunteer groups, in professions or job responsibilities. However, our goals may be unlike these other organizations, because we are a religious, spiritual, rational, inclusive, emotional, spirited community.

> The only safeguard . . . is—in the best Unitarian Universalist tradition—wide participation in a full and complex exploration of the many facets or the problem, and collective struggle to create responses that are complex enough to do justice to ourselves and our community.
>
> —Mary Moore, "Finding Our Way,"
> *Transforming Thought Series, Volume III*

What Sort of Situations Are We Talking About?

We are in the midst of an epidemic of misbehavior that is becoming visible. We probably do not know if the incidence is rising or a societal willingness to break the silence and to believe reports of victimization is revealing a long-standing high rate. We do know our startlement when not only professionals, but also family members, friends, and colleagues are found to be violent, betraying, exercising power-over, or simply acting unwisely.

—Betty Hoskins, "Comforting the Bystanders and Cleansing the Religious Community," *Edge of the Wave*

As leaders encounter a potential problem, ask:

- What sort of problem is this? Is the situation a tangle of misunderstandings, a breach of professional behavior, an allegation of gross sexual misconduct?
- Are we trying to avert a legal liability?
- Are we trying to prevent harm to a child or an adult?
- Are we presented with a need to respond to a situation, for example, clergy misconduct in our or a nearby church, inappropriate advances by a newcomer, or a long-smoldering disagreement between respected members?
- Are we working to heal an old embedded wound that remains within this church's history, perhaps even unidentified?
- Are we working to heal a wound brought in with the people who bring their complex lives to this congregation?
- Have we involved all the appropriate persons and committees?

We are focusing on three kinds of situations:

1. Clergy sexual misconduct and abuse. In the last few years, people in the congregations, affiliated women's organizations, and professional leadership of the Unitarian Universalist Association have had to deal with a variety of difficult situations involving clergy. Such situations included multiple affairs with counselees, and "conduct unbecoming" (such as entering a new relationship while still in a committed relationship, and a felony conviction for statutory rape).

Unethical and inappropriate behaviors by clergy have grievous results in congregations. They are not only breaches of professional code, boundary violations, and abuses of power over someone, they also cause the loss of trust that congregations need to bind them into religious communities.

> [The concept of affected bystanders] takes us one final step toward broadening our vision. It takes us beyond the dyadic focus of clergy-parishioner to include the larger community affected but often effectively without voice. . . . "Bystanders" suggests a fundamental tension between two distinct ways of understanding the sexualization of relationships by clergy: Is sexual misconduct by clergy best understood as a moral failing to be dealt with on an individual basis or a question of collective concern, requiring a more public integration into our theological and ethical life as a religious community?
> —Susann Pangerl, "An Invitation to Readers," *Edge of the Wave*

When a committee on ministry or a board charges clergy misconduct, it must take care to ensure fairness, to determine the accuracy of the charges, and to protect both the victimized and the accused. And care must be taken to preserve the community, both locally and farther away.

But fairness can be used unfairly. When a person—most often a woman—brings a charge of sexual misconduct against the minister, some boards have felt the fair way was to ask the victim to appear before the board with the accused present. They defend this practice by citing the legal principle that an accuser must face the accused with the charge. A solution that seems totally fair to the board can be harmful to the victim.

> Because of these harmful practices and habits, the victim, almost always a woman, rarely gets the chance for a hearing and healing. All too often, the victimizer's fellow clergy will call for peace, not justice. We don't blame them for wanting the incident and the victim to go away, but it doesn't go away until justice is done. It lives on in the life of the victim and undermines the trust and safety of the congregation.
>
> —Phyllis Rickter, "Women Speak Out," *World*, January/February 1993

Such a board process, based on legality rather than reality, right rules rather than right relations, reveals ignorance of the victim/perpetrator dynamic, the differing socializations of women and men, and the power of the ministry, and so further harms the woman. Each victim needs an advocate to ensure fairness.

In fact, all of us need leadership help in making sense of the events. We are all bystanders, whether we are in the local congregation, in nearby churches, or affected by negative news about our religious affiliation. We need opportunities for openness and for active affirmation of the Purposes and Principles.

2. Peer harassment and abuse. As the Unitarian Universalist Women's Federation, the Women and Religion Committee, two task forces, and various ministerial organizations grappled with local situations of clergy misconduct and abuse, there arose—predictably—questions about parishioner behavior, lay power, and lay responsibility. As laypeople and ministers immersed in American and Canadian cultures, we bring assumptions and behaviors that we've only begun to reevaluate.

In the Unitarian Universalist atmosphere of openness and acceptance, is any behavior out of bounds? How often do we hear, "Oh, he doesn't mean a thing by that; he's harmless." "She comes on to everyone." "Cruising is normal in their lifestyle." That sounds as if every person is on their own to defend herself or himself against harassment. What is leadership's role in setting limits?

Sexual innuendo or abuse are not the only hurtful behaviors. In an era of sound bytes and rapid "startle reaction" judgments, how do we disagree without feeling unsafe with each other? Do we silence people who state unpopular views? Hard as it is, leaders need to take the time to sit down and actively listen, actively paraphrase, actively synthesize a variety of people's thoughts.

How do we support leadership in difficult tasks? We expect board members and ministers to find the courage and the skill to confront difficult people and difficult issues appropriately. For the sake of safety in the congregation, we expect our leadership to make it clear that we object to inappropriate and unwelcome words, touching, and assumptions of intimacy.

Equally, we object to rude and judgmental exchanges at meetings. Many congregations are starting Safe Congregation committees that stimulate a dialogue on the range of appropriate behaviors, the difficulties of interpreting each others' intentions, and ways to value each other.

3. Child abuse or neglect. We often assume the children in our religious community are safe, an assumption that may be regrettably erroneous. Some people attracted to our congregations think our openness and acceptance guarantees that we'll meet their needs. Does every person have the right to teach church school? Are written guidelines clear about the behavior of adults working with children? (See information about the Department of Religious Education's Safety/Abuse Packet in the resources section of this book.) We suggest making it clear that the focus of the children's religious education program is the children, not the adults' needs for the companionship of children.

On a wider scale, most of us were raised in harsh and less-than-effective ways. We know there are neglectful and abusive parents in our midst. We may feel religious and ethical responsibility to these parents and their children, but how can we intervene without offense?

Is action solely the responsibility of religious professionals? In each state or province, is there a legal obligation to report suspected abuse? If so, will the board and religious education committee be notified? What follow-up should lay leadership provide?

Can a Unitarian Universalist congregation have a different atmosphere, a culture different from the surrounding world, a safer culture? Is that not one reason we came here? Have we not chosen a non-creedal, non-dogmatic faith, joined in our Unitarian Universalist Purposes and Principles?

Questions of authority are a major part of our puzzlement. What sort of problem is it? What sort of remedy is needed? Who should exercise authority? Who gave us, or the minister, authority? Again, the mix of models can be confusing and may need untangling.

The nature of authority is often fuzzy for Unitarian Universalists. Our local governance (or polity) means there is no top-down assignment, no bishop, no delegation, no final authority above. Who, then, called us to do this work?

Ministers are called by congregations; they identify an internal calling to pursue studies and develop professional and spiritual skills of ministry. By ordination, they have, in the eyes of the world, authority. At the same time, a minister's authority is derived in large part from our calling him or her to be our spiritual leader.

Who gives authority to board and committee members? We do, by installing them with our congregational charge, by voting and ratifying votes, and by having an annual meeting. The state, commonwealth, or province also conveys authority.

Power is equally complex. Top-down, delegated power is the model in most civic organizations—and most religious organizations. The ability to deny and to punish is as strong as the ability to teach and foster self-esteem. As Unitarian Universalists, we speak of empowerment, of calling forth the strengths and abilities within everyone.

Even more, most of our theological images place us in a benign or indifferent universe, without an angry God or Lord or king. Our Purposes and Principles say we act democratically, with regard for minority opinions.

Leadership includes truth-telling. We may know that breaking silence is the beginning of healing, but also fear the community will feel unsafe. We may wonder, is truth-telling worth the trouble it may cause? How often we are urged to let sleeping dogs lie, to move on to the present, to negotiate a settlement that "pays the debt to society."

When we are trying to tell the truth, we are concerned about confidentiality and gossip. However, too often confidentiality becomes secrecy and protects the powerful. Too often, the accusation of gossip prevents us from validating the story of a real person's life.

Dealing forthrightly, while acknowledging complex questions, yields gratitude and allegiance. Involve the congregation, reaching as full a group as possible, as soon as possible. In the initial stages, while accusations are investigated, respect privacy; but many people will know. There will be rumors. Positions will be taken. There will be personal reactions on the basis of each individual's past, private life experiences. Use the opportunity for clarifying hopes for justice in this ongoing community. Use the Purposes and Principles as affirmations of diversity and sound judgment.

So we suggest. Effective Unitarian Universalist congregational leadership finds time to think through questions of authority, power, and truth-telling; has open discussions among minister, staff, and laypeople; knows when to ask for help and information; and knows it does not have all the answers. An effective board knows there are sources of information and help; a proactive board reduces risk and develops its right relationships by asking for input.

Leadership in a Unitarian Universalist congregation, both ordained and lay, reflects on and models and improves ways of being together. This is what drew us to this religious movement. How can we build and sustain a safe congregation and right relationships? What can we count on from each other, here in Unitarian Universalist congregations?

In approaching a specific situation, leadership asks questions such as:

- When and how is the minister involved? Is this a pastoral matter that the minister should initially handle or do we need a solution to a congregational problem, with the minister as a partner in decision making?

- Is this an infraction of congregational policies, procedures, rules, or bylaws?
- Is this a pastoral or ministerial matter involving a vulnerable or unbalanced person? Is this an issue of human aspirations, to be addressed in sermons?
- Are children at risk?
- Have laws been broken?
- Does the situation involve a minister's behavior? Is there a break of the promises or covenant the congregation and minister made to each other when they called and accepted ministerial leadership?
- Does the situation involve laypeople's behaviors? Is there a break of the community covenant?
- What activities and attitudes respond to past wrongs and lead to healing?

But remember, the church board and the staff have legal responsibility as well as religious/spiritual obligations. Boards have an obligation to reduce risk to the institution. Legal liability can lie ahead for boards that do not understand their responsibility for the actions of those they supervise or employ. For example, does one's state or province mandate that professionals must report child abuse when they discover it? Check what agreement there is with religious education professionals. Often boards must seek outside counsel in situations that have legal implications.

What do we do with a conflict between legal and ethical obligations? We trust boards to be prudent and also to take seriously the ethical obligations of a religious community. Frequently a clash of values erupts. For example, some people defend free speech; some people say that safety in the congregation is more important. How can we avoid such either/or situations where we apparently are being urged either to set aside our ethical-religious standards or to be unlawful?

How can we reframe the question so that both spiritual and legal aspects are satisfied? Arrange for a service on right relations, an adult education session, and/or a sermon that deals with both rights and responsibilities, reason and spirit, the ethics of caring and the ethics of justice. Ask about the experiences of other leaders. What experience can we draw upon? What are the roles of district leadership?

As a result of the past five-plus years of grappling with clergy misconduct, the roles of district leadership have become clearer, and experienced persons and teams are in place. Congregational leadership should use this system and suggest places where it may need modification. Effective boards know when to seek counsel and are comfortable using it. They ask many questions—ethical, legal, spiritual—to handle difficulties with grace and fairness.

The Good Offices Person, appointed by the Unitarian Universalist Ministers Association, is an ordained colleague of the minister, and stands with, counsels, and supports ministers in handling issues of controversy between the minister and the congregation. A Good Offices Person is also appointed by the Liberal Religious Educators' Association to support and advocate for colleagues in religious education in issues of controversy and conflict within the congregational setting.

In addition, most UUMA chapters have clergy teams trained in dealing with issues related to clergy sexual misconduct. The model developed by the Reverend Dr. Marie Fortune, a United Church of Christ minister and founder of the Center for the Prevention of Sexual and Domestic Violence, has been adapted for much of their training. Most UUA districts are forming a Safe Congregation Team of clergy and laity.

A variety of services is provided by the Unitarian Universalist Association with your Annual Program Fund dollars. Congregational polity requires that we ask for their services, programs, and expertise. Ask! The phone number is (617) 742-2100. The address is 25 Beacon Street, Boston, MA 02108. See the resources section in this book for information on UUA departments, professional organizations, and affiliated organizations.

We all have reasons to doubt, to lose hope, to despair of the effects of our own and other peoples' behaviors. But instead we choose right relationships in the same way we choose life. We can choose to act as if people can be good, and we can treat them as we wish them to be. Not blindly, not foolishly, but with hope—we do this knowing that human beings are complex and that a complex world contains many blocks to reaching our goal.

In community, in right relations, and in building safety in our congregations, we extend the struggle into the rest of our lives.

Cases of Misconduct and Abuse

1. Clergy Sexual Misconduct and Abuse

After their minister is removed from fellowship and ministerial duties because of proven "conduct unbecoming," some members of a congregation travel afar to try out other Unitarian Universalist churches. Their behaviors are varied, as is the welcome they receive. Some don't want to talk about what happened in their previous church for fear of losing friends and experiencing more trauma. Others want it out in the open; indeed they cannot stop raising the issue and demanding help from the district and from UUA headquarters. Some, who have been valuable, active participants, say they'll never join a church again. If these folks visit your congregation:

_____

- What can or should your local church leadership do?

- Which committees and individuals would have responsibilities?

- Who would advocate for each party?

- What services would you seek from the district and the UUA?

- What are local resources (shelters, hotlines, community and legal organizations)?

- What resources does the congregation contain (members who volunteer at shelters, hotlines, and organizations—therapists, social workers, professors, nurses, health care providers, substance abuse counselors, physicians; members with business and legal experience, and others)?

2. Child Neglect or Abuse

A parent volunteers to teach in the church school. You discover that this person must have supervised visits with his or her own child because of previous findings of abuse. Some members feel this person has been punished enough by enforced supervision of their family, and argue that the church should not place restrictions on someone who is trying to reform.

_____

- What church leadership groups (board, committees, staff) should be involved in discussions and decisions?

- What procedures should be in place? What additional policy and procedures would you argue for?

- What does leadership communicate to this parent?

3. Peer Harassment and Abuse

A person who has been attending a congregation for only a month is very sociable at the coffee hour. The person hugs, embraces, pats everyone he or she wishes to. Some people find the behavior amusing; some find it repulsive; some find it embarrassing and say they'll stop attending the congregation unless something is done.

How would you rate this hugging behavior? acceptable, not acceptable, in a gray area? requiring or not requiring board or committee action?

The agenda of the next board meeting calls for discussion of what action is needed, if any. The meeting gets heated. One woman is told she's hypersensitive and doesn't know how to take a joke. One man is told he's insensitive and never takes anything seriously. Both leave the meeting feeling unheard.

- What church leadership groups (board, committees, staff) should be involved?

- What procedures should be in place?

- What additional policy and procedures would you argue for?

The matter is referred to the Safe Space Committee, who try working with the following diagram, a range of behaviors on a continuum drawn by Dr. Bobbie Groth.

Continuum of Abuse

ABUSE is the misuse of power in a relationship to hurt or control.

PHYSICAL  DEATH

pushing punching slapping kicking throwing objects choking using weapons homicide/suicide

VERBAL
EMOTIONAL  SUICIDE

name-calling criticizing "you're no good" ignoring yelling isolation humiliation

SEXUAL  RAPE

unwanted touch visuals unwanted looking sexual name-calling unfaithfulness
false accusations forced sex hurtful sex

Without some kind of help, the violence usually gets worse.

DEATH can ALWAYS be the result.

Adapted from VILLAGE TO VILLAGE, Alaska Dept. of Public Safety.

While this problem is being referred, what does leadership do to address the congregation's concerns? If the group is inclined to dismiss verbal and emotional items, know that recent research shows that it escalates to physical abuse within one year in 76 percent of incidents.

Some members of the congregation object that this approach, even when customary or necessary, focuses the discussion on "can's and can'ts." Such line seeking may be read as a search for permission for continuing undesirable actions. What's the alternative? In addition, this group doesn't want to prohibit physical conduct; they like to greet each other with warmth. Where does hugging fit? The Safe Space Committee tries out answers by using another continuum.

We live in a continuum (or circle) of qualities of relationships. Try drawing this continuum as a circle: acquaintances, shared events, shared social causes, confidantes, active listeners, those we are attracted to (whether we act on that attraction or not), affairs, long-term relationships (marriages, partnerships, committed relationships).

What parts of the circle can be considered in congregational life? When are leadership, laypeople, staff, and clergy involved?

4. Congregational Polity

The Unitarian Universalist Association is an association of congregations whose member congregations, through the Annual Program Fund, make financial contributions that support programs that are in turn made available to the members. In her essay, "An Ethic of Right Relations," in Session 1, Deborah Pope-Lance describes "a congregation [who] objects to the Association's requirement that they make a minimum financial contribution in order to receive the Association's services and staff support." A decision to cease support of the Association is extreme and would presumably require careful consideration. Yet it is one alternative. After all, as Pope-Lance concludes: "The rule of congregational polity is fundamental to the liberal church."

• What are the issues for a congregation facing this possibility?

• What are the leadership responsibilities in a congregation considering this alternative? to the members? to the district? to the UUA?

• What other responses are available to congregational leaders facing this issue?

• Is there a leadership role for a cluster? the district? a neighboring congregation? an area UUMA chapter?

• What are the effects for a congregation facing this possibility?

5. Anti-racism

Two delegates return to their suburban congregation from a General Assembly that included a day's focus on racism. They are excited by the programs and possibilities they've heard about, eager to share what they have learned, and ready to commit their time to an agenda the UUA has recommended to all its congregations. On Sunday they give their delegate's report and suggest that the congregation affirm and support the anti-racism priorities as voted by the General Assembly. They are surprised and disappointed that the congregation is not more enthusiastic about this initiative. Those attending the meeting tell the delegates that the Principles and Purposes and their congregation's mission statement already make clear they are anti-racist; besides, they have tried for years to welcome people of color and have met with little success. These people suggest that there's nothing more that can be done, that it is better to turn the congregation's energy and attention to other important issues.

- Where should the congregational leadership for this issue come from? the social justice committee? religious education? music committee? an ad hoc group? the governing board? the minister?

- What are the other sources of leadership (other than the congregation)?

- Has your congregation (or one you are familiar with) had a similar situation? How was it resolved?

- How would your congregation respond to its General Assembly delegates if they made a similar presentation? Would the response be different if an appeal for participation came from the minister? the president? a UUA staff person?

- As a group, or in small teams, outline how you might present the case for an anti-racism agenda for your congregation.

3 Abusing a Sacred Role

Goals	• To explore the issues of clergy sexual abuse and misconduct
	• To share expectations of the clergy-congregant relationship
	• To review congregational, district, and Unitarian Universalist Association resources and guidelines regarding clergy sexual abuse and misconduct.

Goals

- To explore the issues of clergy sexual abuse and misconduct
- To share expectations of the clergy-congregant relationship
- To review congregational, district, and Unitarian Universalist Association resources and guidelines regarding clergy sexual abuse and misconduct.

Materials

- One copy of the discussion essay for each participant
- One copy of Resource 6 for each participant
- Appropriate congregational material: safety policy, committee descriptions, Committee on Ministry covenant, or mission statement
- Copies of *Singing the Living Tradition*
- Chalice or candle and matches

Preparation

- Distribute the discussion essay to each participant with instructions to read it before the session begins.
- Read the discussion essay by Deborah Pope-Lance before the group meets.
- Review the case study in Resource 6.

Session Plan

Gathering and Centering   5 minutes

Light the candle or chalice and read "Affirmation," reading no. 470 in *Singing the Living Tradition.*

Check in with participants by inviting questions and comments from the previous session or from their reading of the discussion essay.

Focusing   5-10 minutes

Read the goals for this session with the group.

If this is the first gathering of participants for Creating Safe Congregations work, establish group guidelines. Refer to page 10 for the procedure.

Reflection 10 minutes

The Unitarian Universalist ministry is a unique calling and profession with a special relationship to a congregation. In *Awakened From the Forest*, Robert Karnan gave voice to these qualities in his meditation "Shared Ministry."

> What makes my experience in the ministry so hopeful for me is that I am not alone in this careful hearing of both pain and excitement. This is not something reserved for only one ordained and robed. It is something we all do for and with one another.
>
> Ours is a shared ministry, a giving and receiving. We tell one another our stories, our myths, our innermost thoughts—and we seek to listen (if we can) with sensitivity and purpose and love.
>
> We live lives. We do not live creeds or theologies or even values. We are engaged with real events and people, and we are related, torn, and isolated together. We are at odds and we are sometimes very close.
>
> The spiritual center of our lives is not to be found in a faith, no matter how cherished or revered. It comes, rather, out of the openness and honest engagement, the courage and pain, and the love we experience with one another. Sometimes that openness is searching and doubting, confused or serene, ambivalent or empowered. But it is an openness nonetheless.
>
> And out of it comes a vision of a world made new by the reality of our lives, lived in the service of love and justice, of gentle goodness and forgiveness.
>
> A minister seeks to live in the struggle of each and every one of us as we seek to come to an understanding of who we are, where we are, how we are. A minister seeks to help us raise up the vision of where we must go as a people, and invites us if we need the invitation to join hands and hearts with one another to get there.
>
> This shared ministry is dependent on two factors: great congregations (whether large or small) and effective, dedicated ministers. The most important feature of their relationship is that they create one another.

Ask members to respond to Karnan's thoughts.

Exploring 75 minutes

Turn the group's attention to the discussion essay. Pope-Lance raises three critical issues in relation to clergy sexual abuse and misconduct. Discuss each.

1. "Sexualized behavior with parishioners is an abusive misuse of professional power. . . . It is always the minister's responsibility to use his or her power ethically and to maintain the professional role." Why is it always the minister's responsibility?

2. "Dual relationships are in conflict and increase the likelihood of unethical conduct." What sort of congregational and clergy boundaries might be crossed or violated in dual relationships? Why might these be a problem, "increase [ing] the likelihood of unethical conduct"?

3. "Ministerial misconduct is wrong because it takes advantage of the vulnerable." Who are the vulnerable in a congregation and why?

Finally, if time allows, talk about the statement: "Ministerial misconduct . . . betrays the most precious principles upon which a religious community is based." What are the principles she speaks of and why is their violation a betrayal?

Now pass out Resource 6 and discuss the following questions:

- Pope-Lance says that misconduct is often characterized as a personal problem, unlawful, sinful, negligent. How would you characterize the misconduct in this case study? Why?
- As Pope-Lance suggests, discuss the power and authority issues of the case, giving attention to issues of vulnerability, secrecy, and control.
- How might this case have been handled differently?
- What process does your congregation have for responding to issues of ministerial misconduct?
- In your congregation, what are congregational and ministerial problem areas and issues that might relate to misconduct and abuse?

  Minister related: counseling contexts, isolation, dating, educational opportunities (e.g., participation in the UUMA sponsored workshops on clergy misconduct).

  Congregation related: displays of affection (hugging, kissing, touching), a clear process for staff and members to raise or report unethical behavior, awareness of the staff's responsibilities.

Integrating   15 minutes

At the end of her essay, Pope-Lance concludes: "There is nothing . . . more spiritually death-dealing than the failure of a religious community to insist on an integrity of religious values and action."

How do the Unitarian Universalist Association and your congregation move toward insisting on this integrity?

How might you participate in maintaining this integrity?

Closing   5 minutes

Gathering around the candle or chalice, ask participants for any insights, reflections, or closing thoughts.

End with a reading of Susan Manker-Seale's "Benediction" from *Awakened From the Forest:*

Much of ministry
    is a benediction
A speaking well of
    each other and the world
A speaking well of what we value:
    honesty
    love
    forgiveness
    trust
A speaking well of our efforts
A speaking well of our dreams
This is how we celebrate life
Through speaking well of it
Living the benediction
    and becoming as a word
        well-spoken.

Evaluation and Planning

Consider the following questions. Reflect on them and discuss them with your co-leader(s).

1. How do I feel about this session now?
2. What was good or not so good about this session? Why?
3. If I were to lead this session again, what would I do differently?
4. What preparations do I need to make for the next session?

Preying on the Faithful: Ministerial Misconduct by Sexual Abuse

Deborah J. Pope-Lance

My subject is a difficult one that some may find unpleasant and upsetting. But it is an important and unfortunately not unfamiliar topic. In the last several years, newspapers and television journalists have reported on ministers and priests who have been accused or convicted of engaging in sexual behavior with those whom they have been called to serve.

The Reverend Jim Bakker of Praise The Lord ministries was ousted from his position as spiritual and corporate head of that organization. Jimmy Swaggert, repentant and sobbing, confessed to the sin of adultery on live television. Father James Porter was convicted in two states for sexual assaults on children in his charge. And Father John Hanlon received a life sentence for similar behavior.

These clergy, in the course of their pastoral duties, engaged in sexual behavior with members of their congregations. Their behavior violated the ethics of their profession and sexually abused people who had come to them expecting counseling and care. Instead of praying for them, these clerics preyed upon their faith.

Father Porter was convicted of sexually abusing numerous children, almost entirely young boys, during his tenure as a priest in southeastern Massachusetts. Nearly 30 years ago, long before he left the priesthood, his unethical behavior had been known by some of the church's leadership. Rather than removing him from the priesthood, the church moved him from parish to parish, providing him with additional opportunities to abuse persons in his charge. Eventually he was encouraged through counseling and administrative incentives to re-enter secular life, but not until his victims numbered in the dozens.

The Reverends Bakker and Swaggert had sexual relationships with women who worked in their churches or were prostitutes. Both men were married and considered righteous and faithful, pastors whose care and wisdom aided others in avoiding sin. Swaggert was silenced for a year. Both men eventually resumed their ministries.

Sexual abuse and misconduct by clergy is not a new problem. In the middle of the nineteenth century, Horatio Alger, minister of the First Parish in Brewster, Massachusetts, resigned his pulpit and fled to Europe for repair and convalescence. According to the parish records, he had been caught "doing unspeakable things in the balcony" with little boys. Thereafter, Alger made his living as a correspondent and author, writing stories of young boys from humble beginnings who pulled themselves up by their bootstraps and despite great obstacles became successes. Both Alger's victims and his novel's heroes were prepubescent boys.

In the 1870s, Henry Ward Beecher, pastor of Brooklyn's Plymouth Congregational Church for 25 years and considered by many to be the greatest preacher in America at the time, was accused of having a sexual liaison with Elizabeth Tilton, a prominent member of his church and the wife of one of his closest friends. There had been others. Beecher, as an important and influential voice in the abolition and suffrage movements, called upon his friends to defend him. While he had violated Victorian standards of morality and evidenced a damning hypocrisy, their defense saved his ministry. No one ever questioned his professional ethics or suggested that he had been negligent in his pastoral duties to these women, his parishioners.

What makes the behaviors of these clerics unethical? What makes sexual relationships or sexualized behavior with parishioners professional misconduct and negligence?

The abuse is often seen by parishioners, colleagues, and denomination officials as a personal problem—difficulty with alcohol, emotional disturbance or illness, addiction, a parish conflict, adultery, or a violation of celibacy vows. Newspaper articles about Bakker and Swaggert spoke of the sin of adultery and noted that while the spirit was faithful, the flesh had been weak. The reports of Archbishop Marion of Atlanta recounted the tragedy of a cleric who was unfaithful to his priestly vows. Surprisingly, little mention was made of the victim's tragedy, of the women exploited by powerful men. The women were characterized as greedy prostitutes, hysterical church women, or spurned and vengeful lovers. Fathers Porter and Hanlon were described as "sick," as men whose natural sexual feelings and urges were repressed by an inherently anti-sexual and anti-female religion and perverted into pedophilic behavior.

Ministerial misconduct no doubt is evidence of a personal problem, but it is not only or most importantly this. Pedophilia is unlawful. Adultery is considered sinful by communities of faith and neither admirable nor honorable by the general public. When these behaviors are engaged in by a minister, however, in the course of his or her routine pastoral duties and relationships, they are not merely unlawful or sinful, or without honor, they are negligent, improper, and a professional problem. A minister's professional relationships presuppose certain roles and expectations. To the faithful, a minister provides spiritual resources and direction, care and counseling. A minister is expected to use his or her expertise and knowledge to serve the best interests of a parishioner. Sexual behavior or contact is not part of the pastoral role. Such behavior may be expected in a relationship between lovers, but not between a minister and person with whom he or she has a pastoral relationship. What Porter and Hanlon did with their victims was abusive, not only because it involved the rape and sexual assault of children, but because Porter and Hanlon violated their pastoral roles and duties in relation to these children.

A minister's sexual involvement with a parishioner is not primarily a matter of sex or sexuality, but of power and control. Rape and sexual assault are acts of violence not because they are sexual, but because they offend, control, and injure their victims. The means by which the other is overpowered and hurt is sexual, but it is not this means that makes the action violent or abusive.

Sexualized behavior with parishioners is an abusive misuse of professional power. The role of a minister carries with it authority and the responsibility to use it to benefit the people he or she serves. When a minister uses this power to pursue sexual contact or relationship, it is an abuse of power and responsibility. Even when a parishioner initiates a sexual relationship, it is always the minister's responsibility to use his or her power ethically and to maintain the professional role. Employing the power, responsibility, and trust they held because of their ministerial positions, Beecher, Bakker, and Swaggert initiated or pursued sexual relationships with women and then attempted to silence or disparage them to cover up for their own misconduct. Through the exercise of their power over and access to these women, they used and injured them for their own gratification without regard to these women's feelings, needs, or vulnerabilities.

While much has been reported recently of sexual abuse and misconduct by psychologists and psychiatrists, these and other types of therapists have articulated in their professional codes and licensing statutes their understanding that therapy involves a specific and defined relationship with clients. Becoming friends, starting a business, or developing a romantic relationship outside the therapy are inappropriate and create a greater likelihood of unethical conduct. Ministers who often live in communities with their parishioners and have less clarity about the specific boundaries and limits of their professional roles develop, in the routine course of their pastoral work, dual relationships. In addition to being a pastor, a minister may be a friend, a supervisor, a teacher, an administrator, a fellow parent, and a neighbor. These dual relationships at times are in conflict and increase the likelihood of unethical conduct. Sexualizing relationships with people one has a pastoral and professional role with violates the boundaries and limits of that role. If a pastoral relationship pre-exists between two people who see themselves as consenting adults, as equals, it is the minister's responsibility to honor the duties of that role and to take steps to prevent the development of a sexual relationship.

Ministerial misconduct by sexual abuse is unethical and wrong because it takes advantage of the vulnerable. A ministerial relationship is a sacred trust, a place where people can come with their deepest wounds and vulnerabilities and expect they will be offered healing, not additional injury. Tremendous harm is done when vulnerabilities are exploited. A person's mental health, sense of self, and spiritual well-being may be devastated for many years. When a minister sexualizes a relationship with a parishioner, he or she takes away the church's appropriate, powerful, and sustaining spiritual guidance and support and robs the victim of the spiritual care and creativity the church has intended and ought to provide. He or she violates a fundamental religious principle: to protect the vulnerable and to heal the broken.

When ministerial misconduct occurs, everyone loses. Many victims not only despair for the loss of their religious community, they also feel as if their souls have been stolen. They often lose their trust in all clergy, sometimes their reputations, even their friends and jobs. Congregations are left to cope with feelings of betrayal and rage. They must sort out the confusion they feel for the minister they trusted and valued and the minister who violated their trust and caused harm. Disillusioned and discouraged leaders must reckon with disgruntled and traumatized members and the chaos of a spiritually and financially devastated organization.

Ministerial misconduct violates not only professional ethics and standards of good practice, it betrays the most precious principles on which a religious community is based. Churches are intended to be communities of faith where the inherent worth and dignity of persons is honored and respected, where each person, a child of God according to biblical witness, is held safely and in God's care. When abused by a minister, a victim's inherent worth and dignity are disregarded and violated and the foundations of religious faith are betrayed.

After ministerial abuse has occurred, the most compelling religious issue must be justice. Churches are by principle and purpose communities that further peace, compassion, and fairness. Churches must speak and hear the truth. They must name the abuse and condemn it as wrong. Creating safe and just communities requires that churches offer compassion and protection to victims and that they confront and impose negative consequences to the ministers who abuse their sacred trust and responsibility. There can be no healing without justice. For without justice, without an integrity of religious principle and action, hypocrisy will weaken and destroy our churches.

Churches and church officials have been slow to respond but recently have shown a greater diligence. Encouraged and compelled by expensive lawsuits and settlements, reluctant insurance carriers, and the example of churches and individuals devastated in the wake of ministerial misconduct, officials are more willing now to remove an abusive pastor. Several mainline Protestant churches have instituted preventive education and screening for clergy. The Roman Catholic Church has provided local dioceses with strict procedures for promoting and transferring priests and for responding to allegations of abuse. There is considerable room for more diligent and preventive response. To have a significant effect may take a generation.

There is nothing more tragic than a minister who abuses his or her sacred role, nothing more traumatic to a congregation than the violation of the basic principles of its faith. And there is nothing more spiritually death-dealing than the failure of a religious community to insist on integrity of religious values and action. What hurts the victim most is not only the cruelty of the oppressor, as Elie Wiesel has observed, but the silence and inaction of the bystander. For silence too preys upon the faithful.

For the Good of the Congregation

The following case study is fictitious. It has been constructed out of years of work in the area of clergy sexual abuse and represents a tapestry of familiar strands from many cases.

You belong to a mid-sized Unitarian Universalist congregation in the greater New York area. The church is flourishing in most ways and many people in the congregation attribute this success to the long ministry of their recent minister, a middle-aged, married man with three teenage children, who was recently called to a larger congregation near Boston. When he left the congregation, his wife was coordinator of the Caring Program for elders and shut-ins and his children were active in the youth program.

The congregation enjoyed a successful interim ministry last year, which included finding and calling a new minister. The new minister, a thirty-five-year-old single woman in her second parish (her previous ministry was outstanding), has been in place for six months and the entire congregation feels pleased with the choice.

You were on the search committee for the new parish minister and are a member of the Committee on the Ministry, which consults with her regularly. Last week, an influential member of the congregation, a woman who has been treasurer for five years, came to you in distress to report that she had been told confidentially by a young married woman in the congregation that she had been in a sexual relationship with the former minister for a year before he left. The young woman also had told the treasurer that she knew of two other women who had been sexually involved with him before her, but she could not name those women. The young woman said that she suspected there were yet other women.

As a responsible office holder, you ask the chair of the church board for a private and confidential conversation. The chair is a man, a community leader, editor of the local paper. At your meeting, he is first cordial and affirming for your taking the initiative to contact him. You share with him all that you have been told and ask him what he thinks should be done next. At this point, he is evasive and stalls, saying this certainly is a serious rumor; that, if it is true, it would be extremely upsetting to the congregation and could do serious damage at a time when the new minister is getting settled. The chair asks questions and seems interested. He says that he wants to proceed carefully, that there is a lot at stake and many people who could be hurt, not to mention the congregation as a whole.

At the end of your conversation, the chair still seems vague and asks you to speak with no one about the alleged happenings. As the chair, he says, it is his responsibility, and he will handle the matter. He will call on you if and when he needs you. There is no sense, he says, in alarming others needlessly or risking the spread of rumors. He recalls what a fine leader the former minister had been; he says the rumors are almost impossible to believe. He thanks you again profusely for contacting him and ends the conversation.

Two weeks go by and you have heard nothing, then four weeks, then six weeks. By that time, you are extremely nervous about the issue. The treasurer has called you three times asking what you have done about the rumors she reported. You told her vaguely that things are being looked into but that you are not free to discuss it right now. You have asked her to not mention the rumors to anyone else. The treasurer is clearly impatient with your handling of the matter.

You know that the matter has not been discussed at the recent church board meeting. You call the chair again and ask what is happening. He says he is thinking about the matter, that it is very serious; it must be handled with the utmost discretion. He reminds you forcefully that he wants the matter left entirely in his hands. Please be patient, he pleads.

When you suggest that the board should know the rumors and participate in making decisions about what is to be done, the chair blows up over the phone. He is clearly nervous and angry. In the course of the conversation, he rigorously defends the former minister and hints that you might be making up the rumors you have reported to him. If you are not careful, he says warningly, you will be the one who damages the congregation.

Two days later, soon after your distressing conversation with the chair, the treasurer once again calls you. Completely agitated, she vents her frustration for your ineffectiveness and says, "I wasn't going to tell you this, but one of the other women suspected of having an affair with the former minister is the wife of the chair of the board."

"Does the chair know that?" you ask.

"I don't know," replies the treasurer.

What should you do? What needs to be done for the good of the congregation? To whom do you go now with the story? What are the areas of concern? What are the resources and structures in your congregation that can be activated and engaged in these issues? Beyond the congregation? What will be your role in the process?

As you consider the case, keep in mind the following things:

- What immediate response is called for?

- What people need to be involved?

- What is your role?

- What is the role of the new minister?

- What is the role of the UUA? the Department of Ministry? nearby churches? the district executive? the district Safe Congregations Team?

- Whose interests need to be guarded and how? the reporting victim? the congregation? the alleged offender? the alleged offender's family? the new minister? the chair of the board? other possible victims? yourself? the treasurer? Who else?

- What do you see as the issues that need to be addressed?

- What role do you see for the district Safe Congregations Team?

- What other resources, or resource people, may need to be engaged?

4 A Healthy Religious Education Community

Goals	• To explore the meaning of right relationship in the context of religious education
	• To explore safety guidelines for religious education programs
	• To gain understanding of prevention education programs on child abuse, sexual harassment and exploitation, and interpersonal violence
	• To explore safety and right relationship components for teacher or leader training.
Materials	• One copy of the discussion essay for each participant
	• Copies of Resources 7 and 8 for each participant (as needed)
	• Your congregation's mission statement, covenant, and long-range plans relevant to these issues
	• Your congregation's safety/abuse policies and guidelines (if you have developed them) and procedures pertaining to recruitment, supervision, and reporting
	• Safety/Abuse Clearing House packet from the Unitarian Universalist Association Religious Education Department
	• Curricula and resources from the Unitarian Universalist Association and others from this workbook's bibliography
	• Videos that you have chosen and previewed to use, TV, and VCR. Some suggestions are:
	Preschool: *It's My Body* book
	Primary: *Better Safe Than Sorry II* video
	Intermediate: *Touch* and *A Very Touching Book*
	Youth: *No Easy Answers* video
	Adult: *Hear Their Cries: Religious Response to Child Abuse*
	• Chalice or candle and matches
Preparation	• Distribute the discussion essay to each participant with instructions to read it before the session begins.
	• Read the discussion essay by Patricia Hoertdoerfer and Gretchen Thomas before the group meets.
	• Review the activities listed for the Exploring section of this session. Choose the activity you will be using and familiarize yourself with the resources you will need.

Session Plan

Gathering and Centering   10 minutes

Light the chalice or candle with these words by Donna DiSciullo:

> Come into the circle of love and justice,
> Come into the circle of those seeking wholeness and holiness,
> Come and share in the vision of this community.

Check in by inviting participants to share in a sentence or two what a healthy, safe congregation and religious education community would look like. Begin by summarizing some thoughts and comments from a previous session that may include statements about an open process at board and committee meetings, that conflicts would not be ignored, about support at difficult times, and a process and guidelines for expressing concerns and inappropriate behavior.

Focusing   15-20 minutes

If this is the first gathering of participants for Creating Safe Congregations work, establish group guidelines. Refer to page 10 for the procedure.

Read the following meditation, "Home for the Spirit of the Child," by the Reverend Judith Meyer:

> For we are all aware of the fact that churches and temples
>   are no safer than homes or schools or cities
>   where children are hurt
>   or shamed
>   or minimized in so many ways.
> And if we are to consider
>   how to make our meeting place
>   a sanctuary for the young,
>   this is one good place to begin.
> At the very least,
>   a church can be a place where children are treated
>   with care and respect,
>   where no human harm will ever touch them,
> and where no teachings will lead them
>   to think less of themselves
>   or of others.
> It's basic
>   but it is shocking how often religious institutions
>   have failed to meet the fundamental need.
> What goes on in this sanctuary
>   may be more relevant to children's lives
>   than we know.

If it is true that children pursue
 their own spiritual development
  at an early age,
then we need to ask what role our activities here
 may play in that development.

Use this meditation as a springboard for discussion. Engage participants in a discussion of some of the components of right relations in a religious education context. Refer to examples in the discussion essay as well as the goals for this session.

Reflecting   15-20 minutes

Ask: How did the congregation that Gretchen Thomas served transform crisis and hurting to health and empowerment? Refer to specific parts of the story from the discussion essay.

Engage participants in a discussion of major turning points and elements of transformation toward safety and right relations from the essay. Then, from their knowledge and experience of their congregation, engage participants in a discussion of the opportunities for leadership, education, healing, justice, and ethical action available here to further right relations and safety.

Exploring   50 minutes

Choose from the following activities depending on your needs, resources, and time. Activities in this part can also be excerpted and adapted for teacher-training purposes.

1. Engage participants in a discussion of the following:

   - Definitions of child abuse, harassment, exploitation. Use resources you have gathered, especially *Reducing the Risk of Child Sexual Abuse in Your Church*.
   - Policies of your congregation. Highlight components of YRUU Code of Ethics, UUMA and LREDA Codes of Professional Practice, and, if available, your congregation's safety policy, teacher agreements, etc. Inform participants of state laws and child protective services procedures.

2. Pass out copies of Resource 7 to six volunteers. Ask volunteers to role play each of the three levels of disclosure and discuss appropriate responses after each role play.

3. Pass out copies of Resource 8. Highlight the goals of prevention education. Show and discuss age-appropriate resources that you know and have previewed.

4. Show the video *Hear Their Cries: Religious Response to Child Abuse*

and discuss the response appropriate to your religious education program and congregation. The video is available from the Center for the Prevention of Sexual and Domestic Violence in Seattle, WA.

Integrating   15-20 minutes

Reflect on shared knowledge and common learnings from the discussion essay and from experience in this congregation. Engage participants in a discussion of what children and youth expect from your congregation and religious education program. Discuss and decide on your next steps as well as steps in the coming months and year.

Closing   5 minutes

Invite participants to reflect on the crisis of sexual abuse and interpersonal violence in terms of danger and opportunity. Invite them to share a word or two about how difficult and painful it is to acknowledge and address issues and incidents of child abuse and violence. Also share with one another how renewing and empowering it is to clarify this complex issue and evolve into a more caring and responsible religious community that reflects our highest ideals and deepest values. Invite comments.

Close with these words by the Reverend John Cummins from "Re-weaving the Threads, A Movement Toward Wholeness": "May we never rest until every child of earth in every generation is free from all prisons of the mind, and of the body, and of the Spirit; until the earth and the hills and the seas shall dance and the universe itself resounds with the joyful cry: 'Behold! I am!'"

Evaluation and Planning

Consider the following questions. Reflect on them and discuss them with your co-leader(s).

1. How do I feel about this session now?
2. What was good or not so good about this session? Why?
3. If I were to lead this session again, what would I do differently?
4. What preparations do I need to make for the next session?

It Takes a Whole Congregation to Raise a Child
Patricia Hoertdoerfer, Gretchen Thomas, and others

Courageous leadership by many religious educators throughout the Unitarian Universalist Association has broken the silence and addressed the issues of sexual abuse and interpersonal violence. For more than 25 years, *About Your Sexuality* teachers have engaged young people in discussions to build positive and healthy attitudes and values about their own sexuality and to make responsible decisions about their sexual behavior. Many participants in youth groups, young adult programs, and adult classes have benefited from the sessions offered in *About Sexual Abuse* by Fred and Betty Ward that help break the silence about abusive behavior. These programs advise religious leaders to report immediately to the local child protective services agency when there is an allegation or suspicion of sexual exploitation, abuse, or neglect of children. It is our ethical mandate to protect children.

Religious educators have forged creative partnerships in leading educational programs and empowering their congregations to address and deal with issues of sexual misconduct and sexual abuse. Their steadfast commitment to Unitarian Universalism has compelled them to create a safe environment that protects children and adults from harm and promotes their spiritual growth. Religious educator Cindy Soule and parish minister Ralph Galen exemplify this cooperative leadership in reducing the risk of child abuse, leading the long march to a sexual misconduct and abuse policy, and facilitating the renewal of their congregational covenant. In their article "Healing the Temple" from issue 12 of the 1994 Liberal Religious Educators' *Journal*, they ask critical questions:

> How can we build sufficient awareness and trust to hold our community together in a crisis of the magnitude of clergy misconduct or child abuse? What structures can we put in place to withstand such a storm before it happens? How can we react in a manner consistent with our religious principles? Research and experience tell us that we have in our congregations both victims and perpetrators of sexual abuse. Thus any policies we develop have to acknowledge this possibility and address the question of how to support each individual in his or her spiritual growth, while still protecting the safety of one from another if necessary.

The arduous, time-consuming work by these leaders with their congregations, as well as by many congregations across the continent, is documented in the Religious Education Department Safety/Abuse Clearing House packet. The basic components of effective policy and procedures include:

- a policy statement clearly indicating conduct considered unethical by the congregation and judicatory
- procedures for making complaints. Designate a specific person(s)

within the congregation to whom members can make their complaints.

- procedures that provide for due process in assessing the validity of a complaint
- procedures established to disclose previous complaints, findings, actions at the denominational level.

There are many signs of healthy religious education programs moving toward safe congregations—from shared collaborative leadership to open and respectful discussions dealing with interpersonal violence to welcoming young people into all aspects of congregational life. But no environment is totally free of danger, nor can it be made so; but we can do much to nurture an environment of safety and trust. Often things that are potentially dangerous are also essential to the functioning of the congregational system. Our lifespan religious education programs and congregational worship services are at best experiences of religious intimacy and social empowerment. Yet issues of intimacy and power can diminish as well as enhance our ministry to one another.

The dynamic relationships in lifespan religious education reflect the complexity of relationships in Unitarian Universalist congregations. As leaders and participants in religious education, we need to welcome into our lives people and resources that can nourish and enrich our mutual ministry. Equally important, we need to decide what is toxic to Unitarian Universalist purposes and religious education work and to articulate ways of justice and healing in affirming right relations.

A healthy religious education community can enable us to develop the courage and compassion it takes to recover and move beyond overwhelming pain. It is a place of joy and celebration where the whole congregation is committed to the living promise it makes during a child dedication ceremony, often spoken in words like these:

> We, the people of this congregation,
> Understanding our solemn obligations
> to share in the upbringing of these beloved children,
> Do hereby pledge ourselves
> To promote their welfare
> In mind, body and soul,
> To the end that they may grow
> In beauty, love and truth.

It is a place where religious education leaders, classroom teachers, and Unitarian Universalist families design, pledge themselves to, and take responsibility for each participant's religious education. From a religious education teacher-dedication service at the First Unitarian Universalist Church of San Diego, a litany by Elizabeth Molander Jones celebrates this sacred relationship:

> *Children/Youth:* Thank you for being our leaders. We look forward to spending time with you, having fun with you, and learn-

ing from you. We ask that you remember that we are people in our own right, and we ask you to respect us.

Teachers: We accept the responsibilities of being in the classrooms with our children. We promise to bring enthusiasm, talents, and energies to helping them grow in wise and loving ways. We ask your support in this endeavor. Be there when we need help. Listen to us when we need your ear.

Congregation: We acknowledge and honor the role that you have chosen within our community. We know that this is not something you can do alone. We are all teachers and we will strive to remember that. We are all here to support and help you, each in our own way.

The following stories picture ways to respond to unethical behavior as we care for human souls and move toward right relations and safe spaces. They range from the sexual abuse of children by an active, longtime member of a congregation to a classroom covenant among children, parents, and teachers. May they energize and inspire us to make our religious education programs and religious communities more human, more alive, more creative, more passionate, more loving, and more deeply responsible.

In her sermon, "The Care of Human Souls," the Reverend Gretchen Thomas tells the story of a congregation's worst nightmare—the sexual abuse of children by a longtime, active member. It is a story of how the sexual and spiritual lives of two young men were deeply harmed and how the hope, trust, and sacred nature of the shared community was also violated. It is the story of how ongoing recovery and new strength has evolved from these devastating events.

An energetic, central member of the congregation's senior high YRUU group told youth group advisors that two summers ago David (not his real name) had volunteered to keep house and drive him to school during a week when his parents were out of town. David was a church member who sometimes played the organ, sang in the choir, organized coffee-hour food, and could usually be counted on to help, especially with children's events. David had propositioned the youth sexually. It had been hard for the youth to say no to David that night and the next night. He was so disturbed and embarrassed that for two years he did not tell anyone about it until he had a conversation with a classmate about her ongoing problems from having been sexually abused as a child. As they talked, he realized that David had almost certainly propositioned other teenagers, and some of them could well have been molested. After hearing this story, the youth group advisors and ministers gathered all teenagers past and present to ask about David's behavior with them and to help each other understand and deal with what had happened.

It took several months for the youth group advisors, the parish minister, and Gretchen, the minister of religious education, to make sure that only two young men had been sexually molested during the years David was a member of their congregation. They had to talk with every boy (and their parents) who'd been part of the church in the last seven years.

The church staff eventually learned that David was a registered sex offender with two previous arrests for child molesting. David stopped attending church as soon as the ministers questioned him. For the nine months it took the police to complete their investigation and arrest and convict David, everyone who knew about the case was told by the police to not speak about it with anyone beyond their families. To do so would jeopardize the case.

"This is the worst possible case of 'an elephant in the sanctuary,'" writes Gretchen, "the elephant that many people see and step around, but acknowledge only in whispers behind closed doors. Living with family secrets of this kind is always unhealthy.

"But it did give us time. Time to sort out exactly what had and had not happened. Time to wrench ourselves out of our conviction that somehow we should have known. It gave us time to move through and beyond our intense anger at David's betrayal of our children and of our trusting community. Time to reverse our original impulse to keep these events hidden to protect the victims, even though that would create a festering family secret. It was a point at which those of us with no personal experience with sexual abuse had to trust the wisdom of those who had. It gave us time to educate ourselves about child molesting.

"We were fortunate to have among our members several professionals in this field—counselors, therapists, child advocates, lawyers, parole officers, teachers, and child development specialists. We were also fortunate to have active members who were abuse survivors well recovered from their own trauma and experiences. We turned to them for help and they were magnificent. They never let the church leaders and ministers lose courage, slip into denial, or duck the tough issues. They gave us heart and guidance. They demanded that we emerge from these events a healthier church than before.

"It took us months to understand that everyone needed to know that the congregation was actively assisting the victims and that we were making sure this couldn't happen again. From the first moment we saw our mission as assisting the victims. The survivors of David's abuse needed to have others acknowledge what had happened to them. They needed to hear their families and their church family say publicly, repeatedly, and officially that it was wrong, that it should never have happened, and that in no way was it their fault. We learned real assistance meant helping them see justice done, making sure the young men were not rejected by anyone at church, providing therapy they did not have to pay for, counseling their parents and siblings, and making sure David could never again victimize anyone else at our church.

"One of the first things we did was to recognize how vulnerable any volunteer organization, especially liberal churches who take all comers, are to molesters. We made an all-church policy that there would always be two adults working together with any church-sponsored child or youth activity or group, no matter how small.

"As a religious community, when we truly open ourselves to the depths of such an event, we do not simply go through a big crisis that brings about important changes. We do far more. We open ourselves to the possibility of continued growth and change over many years to come. There never comes a time when we can say, 'Well, that crisis is handled. It's in the past.' Such painful, devastating events offer our congregations a golden opportunity to be transformed, to grow into amazingly strong communities of care that we could not otherwise have hoped to become. It is true that once healed, we are often stronger in the broken places now made whole.

"When we took a stand as a congregation that truly cares for human souls, including those souls betrayed by abusers, many other members who have never shared their own stories and pain of having been sexually, physically, emotionally abused or betrayed or harassed will find the courage to tell their own stories, and will naturally look to the congregation for support and encouragement. Other members whose relatives and friends are recovering from abuse will come to you for advice, support, and prejudice-free understanding. Those who have been betrayed in the past by ministers and youth leaders or by anyone connected to the congregations of their past, will begin to hope and then believe that finally they can find lasting healing from these old injuries and betrayals. And nearby congregations, in the Unitarian Universalist Association and other denominations, will come to you for help with their own related concerns and their own hidden histories.

"By facing and openly discussing the experiences of sexual abuse in our community and by committing ourselves to preventing it in the future, we transformed a number of our congregation's regular programs and policies. The congregation agreed:

- To get to know all the children in their care and support and to attend programming that establishes intergenerational trust and dialog
- To make a habit of watching with full care the relationships that develop with the most vulnerable children at church
- To choose our youth advisors, church school teachers, and child care providers carefully, to raise their consciousness about abuse, to train them well, and to give them massive amounts of ongoing support
- To teach *About Your Sexuality* with seventh and eighth graders and *About Sexual Abuse* with older teens, with the best teachers. We may add a parallel course for parents on 'Raising Whole Children in a Broken World,' and/or offer a Planned Parenthood-sponsored program, 'Let's Talk,' for 10 year olds and their parents.
- To empower search and nominating committees to explore candidates' experiences and beliefs about sexual abuse and to make clear the leadership and wisdom in these areas required of leaders and staff of this congregation
- To designate one person (minister, board president, or other leader) to take on the special, ongoing responsibility of publicly and regularly inviting every person to share concerns about inappropriate be-

havior, no matter how small, so he or she can follow up on them, thoroughly, professionally, and with care for everyone concerned. When members of the congregation know this process is in place and participate in it, they can trust that abuse is so clearly and publicly not welcome in this place that abusers will not risk it here.

- To empower the board of directors to take the lead in making very clear that sexual abuse or misconduct by clergy, staff, or volunteers will not be tolerated and will be prosecuted by this congregation.

"But it is in collective worship and community gatherings that one can feel the sea shift, experience the empowerment and growth taking place, actually see the old prejudices giving way to new understandings. The day David was finally arrested, we could write a letter to our members and friends detailing what had happened and what actions had been taken. The following Sunday, we held a worship service in which three adult members of the congregation spoke about their experiences as survivors of childhood sexual abuse. Some members, especially those who learned about the events for the first time in the letter, came that morning with questions like, 'How could such a devastating thing happen here?' or 'How could David, who was my friend, do this to us?' or 'It's wrong to speak publicly about such unmentionable (or disgusting or violent) things.' People came to church that Sunday with anxieties (Will it be in the papers? Will we lose members? What will people say now about Unitarian Universalism?), with fears (Is this really a safe place for my child?), and with appeals (Tell me what to say to my children.).

"The gathered people watched our young people sitting proudly together, and watched the youth group members light the chalice and speak opening words they had written for the service. They learned the many steps the board, ministers, nominating committee, religious education committee, teachers, youth group, and its advisors had taken. We explained the special age-appropriate, professionally led discussions that would take place that morning in each of the church school classes and the meetings of parents, children, and religious education teachers that would follow the service and the survivors' groups that would meet that night. When they heard the homilies by well-known and respected church members who are survivors of childhood abuse, people's questions changed. They became 'Why is it that in violence we forget who we are?' and 'What is my role in the recovery of our two young people and in the rebuilding of our trusting community?'

"Now, once a year, there is a service that focuses on some aspect of sexual abuse, so that as the years go by and other events cloud the memory of this time, and as new members replace old ones, we will not forget. Each year at this special worship service there is a large bare wreath at the center of the sanctuary. During the closing song everyone is invited to tie a piece of ribbon onto the wreath for anyone they know and care about who has been sexually abused.

"The wreath has become a powerful symbol of the truth that sexual abuse has touched and will continue to touch the lives of many, both inside and far beyond this community. It brings the comfort that in your pain over your, your relative's, or your friend's sexual abuse, you are not alone. Here there is a congregation that takes seriously its care of human souls. When you tie a ribbon on the wreath, you join with others to make a real difference in the lives of real people in this, our broken world, which longs to be made whole."

Creating safe spaces and right relations is an ongoing task in religious education as well as an overarching goal in Unitarian Universalist congregations. One program that bears witness to our theology of hope, love, and empowerment is the Rockford (Illinois) Unitarian Universalist Church, which has declared itself a violence-free zone. The church's young people, with their minister of religious education, Colleen McDonald, led the congregation in pledging their stand against violence and in committing themselves to one of many social responsibility initiatives in the following year. Their pledge pairs Unitarian Universalist affirmations with non-violent commitments:

> In this space, there will be no violence against persons.
> *We affirm and promote the inherent worth and dignity of every person.*
>
> In this space, there will be a commitment to non-violent resolution of conflict.
> *We affirm and promote justice, equity, and compassion in human relations.*
>
> In this space, there will be a voice for reform of organizations and institutions that do violence to groups or individuals.
> *We affirm and promote the right of conscience and the use of democratic principles within our congregations and in society at large.*
>
> In this space, there will be a voice for peace among nations.
> *We affirm and promote the goal of world community with peace, liberty, and justice for all.*
>
> In this space, there will be respect and love for our planet and all its creatures.
> *We affirm and promote respect for the interdependent web of all existence of which we are a part.*

Right relations are identified and defined in religious education programs across our continent in many different contexts. Whether named religious education guidelines or ministry with children or codes of conduct or classroom covenants, they grew out of efforts to put our faith in action. Our young people learn Unitarian Universalist principles and values when linked with concrete references to their own experiences. The young people and the religious education committee of the Community Church of New York City wrote this religious education covenant:

I have a right to be happy,
and to be treated with kindness.
This means that no one will laugh at me,
ignore me, or hurt my feelings.

I have a right to be myself.
This means that no one will treat
me unfairly because of who I am.

I have a right to hear and be heard.
This means that no one will yell,
scream or shout, and my wishes
will be considered in any plans we make.

I have a right to learn about myself.
This means that I will be free to
express my feelings and opinions.

I have a right to be treated this way
and will treat others the same way.

A chorus of religious educators of all ages reminds us: "It takes a village to raise a child. It takes a whole congregation to raise a Unitarian Universalist child."

Child Abuse Disclosures

Level 1: Non-verbal Disclosure

This interaction takes place following a church school class. Rachel is nine years old. She is usually lively and talkative in class, but today she is withdrawn and unusually silent. Now you find her sitting alone during coffee hour.

Teacher: Hi, Rachel. Good cookies, huh?

Rachel: Um-huh. *(Her eyes remain downcast.)*

Teacher: What did you think of class today? Those Ten Commandments are heavy duty on the shoulds and should nots. But I thought it was important to bring them up as part of our Jewish and Christian heritage. What do you think?

Rachel: Nothing. It was fine. *(Her arms are crossed; her body language expresses distance.)*

Teacher: You know, I noticed that when we talked about the Fourth Commandment, you seemed unhappy.

Rachel: Which one is that? *(Glancing at teacher.)*

Teacher: That's the one about honoring your father and mother.

Rachel: Oh, yeah. *(Twisting fingers.)*

Teacher: You know, Rachel, sometimes when people are quiet or look unhappy, it means that they are feeling uncomfortable or scared or angry. Were you feeling any of these things during our discussion?

Rachel: No. *(Biting nails.)*

Teacher: Well, your feelings are important to me. So if you ever do feel angry or scared or upset about anything, you can always talk with me or our minister. Or even if you feel confused and don't know what you are feeling, you can talk with us, too. OK?

Rachel: I gotta go.

Teacher: Bye, Rachel. I'll see you next Sunday.

What do you see? What do you hear? What do you do? Do you:

1. Document your observations?

2. Notify your DRE, MRE, or minister?

3. Have another informal conversation with the child?

Level 2: Non-specific Verbal Disclosure

This interaction takes place following a church school *About Your Sexuality* class on child abuse. Marilyn, a 12-year-old girl, comes up to you after class and wants to talk.

Marilyn: I don't like it when you talk about this child abuse stuff. I hope we don't have to do it again next week. Do we?

Teacher: Well, Marilyn. Thanks for telling me how class made you feel today. I wasn't planning for this to be our topic next week.

Marilyn: Good. Because it was gross.

Teacher: Hmm. What made you feel uncomfortable?

Marilyn: Well, like I said, it was gross. And at first, I couldn't believe that any grown-up would do that stuff with a kid . . . and I felt gross.

Teacher: At first? Then what happened?

Marilyn: (Eyes flash to the floor. She speaks quietly.) Well, then I started to feel kind of creepy, because what you were talking about kind of reminds me of what my uncle does to me.

Teacher: Your uncle? Your Uncle Scott?

Marilyn: Yeah.

Teacher: Marilyn, what does your uncle do, exactly?

Marilyn: Oh, he always wants to sit next to me and to hug me. And sometimes he'll stand next to me and rub himself against me. I don't like it.

Teacher: I can understand how that would make you feel uncomfortable. Have you ever said anything to your parents or uncle about how this makes you feel?

Marilyn: No.

Teacher: Is there a reason you haven't said anything?

Marilyn: It's stupid, I know. He just loves me a lot, that's all. Please, don't say anything, okay? I gotta go.

Teacher: (Calling after her as Marilyn runs out of the room.) Marilyn, if you ever want to talk more about this let me know, please.

What do you see? What do you hear? What do you do? Do you:

1. Document the conversation?

2. Notify your MRE, DRE, or minister?

3. Contact the parents to inform them of your conversation with their child?

Level 3: Verbal Disclosure

This interaction takes place during a rehearsal for the church school play. Tim, a 10-year-old boy, is helping the teacher gather up the costumes. He is particularly talkative today.

Tim: You know, I really like plays.

Teacher: I like plays, too. It's so much fun to dress up and make believe. What do you like the most, Tim?

Tim: I like to dress up, too. I've had lots of practice.

Teacher: What do you mean?

Tim: Oh, we have plays in my neighborhood all the time.

Teacher: Is it fun?

Tim: Oh, yeah. My neighbor, Ed, has this great garage and he has lots of old clothes and stuff. He lets all the kids come over and we play dress up.

Teacher: How do you decide what you'll wear?

Tim: Usually Ed decides. He decides everything. You know, like a director. Sometimes he likes to take pictures of us kids. You know, he even takes pictures of us getting undressed. Is he weird or what?

Teacher: Sounds like it could be kind of weird. How do you feel about it?

Tim: I feel okay when he takes pictures of us dressed up, but I feel kinda weird about it when we're undressed.

Teacher: Have you ever told anyone else about this?

Tim: I told my mom. She said that I must be lying again. My mom really likes Ed and his wife. They're like really good friends with my mom and dad. All the kids really like Ed. Everybody likes Ed.

Teacher: This sounds like a difficult situation, Tim. I want you to know that I believe you, and I would like to help you.

Tim: Help me?

Teacher: Yes. There are some people whose job it is to try and help kids when they are in weird situations. The minister and I are among those people. It's important that we tell the minister about Ed. Would you like to or would you like me to?

Tim: But Mom said it wasn't true.

Teacher: I believe you, Tim. And the minister and I will go with you to talk with your mother about this again. I want to tell her myself that I believe you and that we want to help you.

Tim: Okay. But I think Mom will be mad at you.

Teacher: That's okay. I'm not worried about that.

What do you see? What do you hear? What do you do? Do you:

1. Document the conversation?

2. Notify your DRE, MRE, or minister?

3. File a verbal and written report with child protective services?

4. Talk with the parents about both the disclosure and the report that has been filed?

Goals of Child-Abuse Prevention Programs

Prevention Theory

Four Levels
of Prevention

1. Social Change of Own and
Culture
2. Reduce Vulnerability of Victim
3. Avoidance of Problem
4. Prosecution of Victims

Prevention education works at
level 2. Socially responsible
Unitarian Universalists work
at level 1 to change the violence
and abuse in our society and
culture.

Prevention Components
- Body ownership
- Secrets
- Say "no"
- Touch continuum
- Intuition
- Telling

Prevention Program Criteria
How does the program empower children? It should offer:
- peer support
- training in self-assertion
- help from trusted adult
- accurate information (including assault by known person)
- the chance to practice the empowerment skills
- strategies beyond avoidance techniques.

How does the program use children's problem-solving abilities? Does it:
- offer a chance to participate in the problem-solving process
- enable children to make decisions
- provide realistic, immediate solutions
- permit social interaction and different points of view?

Is material presented in an age-appropriate manner?
- It should take into consideration emotional needs as well as the cognitive and language abilities of children.
- It should provide repetition of major information.

Are the strategies presented realistic, providing children with options rather
than prescriptions or fixed remedies?
- Children should be encouraged to generate several responses to any given situation.
- The message should be that the child is never to blame for sexual abuse.

5

Just Relations

Goals
- To explore the use of justice as a defining characteristic of right relations
- To use the resources and texts as guides for determining right relations
- To explore personal and congregational expectations in a framework of just relations.

Materials
- One copy of the discussion essay for each participant
- One copy of Resources 9 and 10 for each participant
- Your congregation's mission statement, covenant, safety policies, and other congregational texts pertaining to the subject
- Newsprint and markers
- Bibles
- Copies of *Singing the Living Tradition*
- Chalice or candle and matches

Preparation
- Distribute the discussion essay to each participant with instructions to read it before the session begins.
- Read the discussion essay by Fredric John Muir before the group meets.
- Review the activities listed for the Exploring section of this session. Familiarize yourself with the resources you will need and plan accordingly so that you have enough time to complete the exercise.

Session Plan

Gathering and Centering   5 minutes

Light the candle or chalice, and read responsively from reading no. 594, "Principles and Purposes for Us All," in *Singing the Living Tradition*.

Check in by inviting questions and comments from the previous session.

Focusing 5-10 minutes

Read through the goals for this session with the group.

If this is the first gathering of participants for Creating Safe Congregations work, establish group guidelines. Refer to page 10 for the procedure.

Reflecting 10 minutes

In the introduction to his essay, Fredric John Muir says, "Right relationships are just relationships. Justice in a relationship means an appropriate balance of power, fairness, and freedom."

In the group, share reactions and comments to Muir's statement. Encourage participants to use examples.

Exploring 75 minutes

Note: This section encourages participants to explore just relations in a congregational context. The exercise is designed for two different sized groups. With either, 75 minutes is a minimum amount of time to complete the exercise. Please review the process and determine how you might best accomplish the goal.

Invite participants to refer to Muir's essay. As a group, read aloud the essay's case study about Ric and Sylvia (see section 7: Accountability) and let people react to it. (5 minutes)

- For one small group of six or fewer: Ask participants to review the case study using the Just Relations Grid in Resource 10. Applying each aspect on the grid to the case, encourage discussion and make notes on a sheet of newsprint to post as a reference. (Do not discuss the last element, which will be taken up at the end of this section.) (40 minutes)

- For a large group of six or more: Divide into small groups (no larger than four). Assign one or several (depending on the number of small groups) elements on the Just Relations Grid to each group. Ask each group to review the case study using its assigned element(s), looking at how the element of justice, Unitarian Universalist principles, and biblical citations apply to the case study. (Do not study the last element yet. Someone should take notes on a piece of newsprint.) (40 minutes)

Post newsprint so it is visible. If time permits, there can be explanations and clarifications. Focus participants' attention on the Just Relations Grid, looking at the seventh element. Using the Accountability Grid in Resource 9 and congregational documents or texts, discuss how your church's leadership might have responded to the issues raised in this case study. What would it need to respond? (25 minutes)

Integrating
15 minutes

Review what makes for a just relation.

Engage participants in discussion: What makes the process and/or recommendation from the previous exercise a just one? Why is it a step toward right relations? Is anything missing? How would your congregation react to the process you have used and discussed?

Closing
5-10 minutes

Gather around the candle or chalice. From *Singing the Living Tradition*, sing one of the following songs: "Spirit of Life" (hymn no. 123), "Gathered Here" (hymn no. 389), or "From You I Receive" (hymn no. 402).

Close with these words: "Our desire and hope for right relations continues. Our congregations are growing, as are our church schools. Our Association supports us as we explore what it means to be spiritually, culturally, and politically diverse. Our desire for just relations is paramount. We have as our guides the collected experiences and wisdom of the years. Taken together, they form a broad base from which to discuss and explore, respond to and create policy, to practice just relations in a safe congregation. Let it be so."

Evaluation and Planning

Consider the following questions. Reflect on them and discuss them with your co-leader(s).

1. How do I feel about this session now?
2. What was good or not so good about this session? Why?
3. If I were to lead this session again, what would I do differently?
4. What preparations do I need to make for the next session?

Just Relations in a Safe Congregation
Fredric John Muir

" . . . to do justice and to love kindness"—Micah 6:8

We take for granted that our congregations are safe contexts, sanctuaries from the stresses and strains of our work and the eccentric and spiritually shallow requests that a host of attention-seeking groups demand. We look forward to the one or several times a week when we can gather with Unitarian Universalist friends in an atmosphere of right relations, relations that are rooted in and guided by our Principles and Purposes.

We take our congregations for granted—the people, programs, and leadership—assuming that our goals and intentions are right and just. Unfortunately right relations are not always the rule: Unjust relations wear thin the fragile bonds that have tied many congregations together, eroding the confidence of leadership and laity, putting at risk long-standing programs, taxing our Association's ability to respond to the institutional, emotional, and spiritual needs of its members. We need a paradigm, or at the least a starting place, for framing our thinking, discussing, policy making, and expectations of right relations and of how to live with one another in good relationships.

In *Is Nothing Sacred? When Sex Invades the Pastoral Relationship*, Marie Fortune outlines seven elements of justice making that follow any instance of sexual abuse. Although she writes about the church and specifically about clergy misconduct, these elements are adaptable for other institutional settings: Her elements of justice making describe what we expect from a right relationship in our congregations. Right relationships are just relationships. Justice in a relationship means an appropriate balance of power, fairness, and freedom. Justice is a defining characteristic of what is right in a right relationship. In this way, the prophet Micah's directive takes for granted right relations—justice and loving kindness are lasting and meaningful when steadied by the strong roots of right relations, and vice versa.

Fortune's elements of justice making are grounded in the Jewish and Christian traditions, which Unitarian Universalism shares. Our Unitarian Universalist Principles parallel and give substantial and additional meaning to both the Fortune and biblical sources. When relationships—casual, friendly, or committed—are violated, put at risk, or threatened, a just relationship is marred as is the safety and integrity of a community. With Fortune's elements of justice making, the biblical sources, and the Unitarian Universalist Principles as guides, an understanding of just relationships can emerge, be examined and discussed, making our congregations not only safer, but more vibrant and caring religious communities.

1. Acknowledging
Principle: The inherent worth and dignity of every person.
(I Corinthians 3:16)

At the core of the Unitarian Universalist faith tradition is the principle that we "affirm and promote the inherent worth and dignity of every person." This affirmation is not a philosophy of individualism, but a conviction that declares the preciousness and holiness of every person. This valued awareness enters all our relationships.

Cautiously and nervously, a mother told me that her eight-year-old daughter had been touched inappropriately while attending church school. She was unclear if it was an adult or another student who had done the touching—at that moment it didn't matter: She was visibly shaken, deeply concerned, confused, frightened, and angered. "How could this happen to my daughter?" she wanted to know, "This has never happened anywhere else."

She talked; I listened. I didn't try to get to the bottom of the violation: She simply wanted to be heard, to tell her nightmare, to have her fear and anger affirmed. She wanted acknowledgment.

To affirm and promote the inherent worth and dignity of every person is a tall order, but something we have the opportunity to do everyday in every relationship. Acknowledging a person's "divinity" is paramount to a just relationship. In I Corinthians 3:16, Paul speaks of this divinity and sacredness by saying that we are as a temple, a vessel where the Holy Spirit resides. We cannot lose sight of this simply because a person is different or an issue is awkward and we don't want to hear it.

In another story, Theresa had met John at church, became acquainted, and gone out with him. Theresa says that he was a nice guy, but after seeing him a couple of times she decided they weren't for each other. She told John she didn't want to date any more, but just remain church friends. They saw each other on Sundays and eventually, after asking several times, John convinced Theresa to have lunch with him. At some point, as she told of their day together, he touched and manipulated her body in such a way that could only be understood as inappropriate. She was outraged and it wasn't long after that she went to see her minister. Elizabeth and Theresa met several times, but Theresa wasn't satisfied with their conversations: She wanted something more. She wanted John to be away from her; she felt threatened by his presence. Elizabeth arranged, with her board's support, to have Theresa (and John, separately) meet with a panel (Elizabeth, three church members, and an area colleague) and hear (acknowledge) Theresa's feelings.

There was intensive discussion before this meeting about the best way to respond to Theresa's accusation and request, her perception that this relationship had been unjust, since the relationship had originated in the congregation. Whether and how to respond were questions the minister and board asked. By acknowledging Theresa's feelings and in this way affirming her worth and dignity, the congregation, via the panel, reached out to her: They stood by their understanding of a just relationship.

Acknowledging the injustice—a person's reality that a right relationship has been violated—can be as straightforward as listening to their feelings of anger, disappointment, confusion, or fear. Of course, it may mean more. In the congregational context, the recognition that a just relationship has been violated begins with affirming and promoting the inherent worth and dignity of every person. This is a principle of Unitarian Universalism.

2. Compassion
Principle: Justice, equity, and compassion in human relations.
(Luke 4:18)

Understand that those who heard Theresa did not affirm her as a victim, try to rescue her, or plot with her: They were present to hear her feelings, not to judge. They were there to listen and stand with her. The leadership of Theresa's congregation took a bold step for just relations when they chose to acknowledge her feelings. They showed compassion; they chose to be present with Theresa when she was feeling exposed and wounded. Compassion in relations means being with or fully present to another. With compassion, a right relation can be a just one.

"To affirm and promote justice, equity, and compassion in human relations" is a Unitarian Universalist principle that indicates a commitment to stand with those who are hurt, oppressed, confused, frightened—in need of justice. This is our ministry to others, which, similar to what Jesus says in Luke 4:18, is a commitment both pastoral and political. His was a ministry of just relations to the disenfranchised, hurting, and desperate.

Who among us hasn't felt blind, captive, oppressed, and in need of good news? Just relations means establishing a balance of power, fairness, and freedom in a relationship; right relations means justice and equity; a compassionate relationship, being present with another, means sensitivity and caring, indignation and action, both empathy and advocacy.

Krista and Russell, a couple in the process of separating, had made the congregation a context for their disagreements. In particular, their seven-year-old daughter became the focus of a verbal tug-of-war: She was a convenient and passive target for their hostility for each other.

Kurt, their minister, spoke to them both, explaining that their behavior was unacceptable. Krista was frustrated and although she was feeling cornered, Kurt encouraged her to reach out for help. She understood that he was going to give the same message to Russell, who listened to what Kurt had to say, but persisted (and intensified) his harassment of Krista and his contact with his daughter during church (he would visit her during church school class at unannounced and inappropriate times). It wasn't long before the entire congregation was aware of what was going on. Krista was ready to leave the church to avoid contact with Russell and the humiliation she felt from the situation.

Both Krista and her daughter were anxious and embarrassed. Krista was not sure what to do about her relationship with the community. Kurt went to the board and asked to be empowered to intervene on Krista and her daughter's behalf—to stand with them in what had become a very unbalanced and unfair relationship, not only for Krista, but for the congregation. Speaking for the board (the congregation), Kurt spoke to Russell, presenting several alternatives. This conversation was followed by a letter. He explained that the congregation, Krista, and their daughter would not be held hostage by Russell's manipulative behavior. By intervening and standing with Krista, the congregation's leadership affirmed and promoted justice, equity, and compassion in a relationship that was not right.

Compassion means suffering with a person, not only acknowledging, but being with him or her. Being present in a relationship helps make it based in justice, equity, and compassion.

3. Truth-telling

Principle: A free and responsible search for truth and meaning.
(Daniel 13: 1-63 (or Susanna 1-63))

Affirming and promoting "a free and responsible search for truth and meaning" may sound straightforward, logical, and unquestionable: How else would we go about our way of religion? Truth-telling (and truth-seeking) is an element of any just relation. With truth, a relationship can be balanced and fair; with truth, relations can be equal, allowing for freedom; when the truth is accessible, a relationship can have the promise of a just maturity.

Ken (30 years old) was from a large family with brothers and sisters. Since his father's recent violent death as well as the breakup of Ken's marriage, he had been unable to keep a job. He had moved back home with his mother and he had become abusive with his girlfriend and her son. For the family's minister, all of this prompted numerous conversations with family members, several phone calls from a panicked girlfriend, and repeated attempts to counsel Ken into therapy and appropriate behavior, which met with resistance and failure.

Ken's relationships were beginning to unravel: His mother was on the verge of throwing him out; his brothers and sisters wouldn't return his phone calls; his girlfriend had already filed a complaint with the police. Yet Ken was oblivious to it all—he thought his relationships were right, not great, but right. What was missing in Ken's relationships was truth-telling: No one shared with him how they felt. There were repeated affirmations of love, concern, and support, but no one told him the truth: His behavior had become intolerable.

The family's minister suggested a meeting with everyone as an opportunity to share their love, frustration, and concern with Ken. Ken's mother agreed to arrange it. The date was set and before Ken arrived, the group discussed their expectations and fears. When Ken came, he was startled to see the filled office. He was told that it was okay if he left, but first his mother needed to say a few things in the presence of everyone. Two hours later, after an intense sharing, all had heard the message that everyone wanted Ken to get on with his life and they would help in whatever way they could, but they were tired of his abuse and blaming. It was a while before Ken made any significant turn, but that evening of truth-telling was his first step toward a right relationship.

Central to this family's need for a right relationship was its initial unwillingness to tell the truth—each person (and couple) in Ken's web had been unwilling to break the silence that kept the truth from being heard. Where there is difficulty breaking a silence that leads to truth and meaning, there is often denial: "This didn't really happen," "It won't happen again," "No one was hurt," "Those who were hurt deserved it," "It wasn't that bad," "Let's resolve this quietly." For all the good that those who use denial are seeking, the result is a lack of compassion and further injustice, making the truth more elusive. When the silence is broken and the truth is told, a relationship can be made just.

Samuel was a stalker; he went to his minister, William, saying he needed help. He was already in therapy, he'd been in treatment for years— "I'm obsessed with these women," he said, but he refused to elaborate. William was firm, telling him he must stop, that he would not stand in the way of prosecution, he would not hide Samuel's illness.

William was not surprised when Lee, one of his parishioners, came to him asking what she could do about Sam's harassing phone calls and unexpected office visits. "Call the police," William suggested. Eventually she did and the police called William to confirm what Lee had shared.

A week later, a woman called William and explained that a member of his church was stalking her and she was frightened. He asked if he could call her right back. He telephoned Lee, asking if she would be willing to speak with the caller. She agreed. Soon the two women met and eventually pressed charges with two others. Samuel was arrested.

Denial causes, among other dilemmas, isolation. In isolation, fear takes control. Living in fear is living in secrecy, and secrets remove the hope of just relations. Only in truth-telling can right relations be built on a foundation of justice.

The biblical story of Daniel's pursuit of truth to free Susanna from unjust accusations is stirring. Daniel's relentless and steadfast commitment to tell the truth prevented Susanna from death. Likewise, embracing a free and responsible search for truth and meaning will strengthen our commitment to just relations.

4. Protecting
Principle: Acceptance of one another.
(Deuteronomy 10:19)

The Deuteronomic Code was clear: "You shall love the stranger, for you were strangers in the land of Egypt." The stranger among us, in our congregations, is the vulnerable one—that person who might be without friends or defenses, the person who could be unsure or unclear, that person who will be anxious or disoriented, the person who is lost or confused. In other words, the stranger, the vulnerable, might be any of us.

In a just relationship, we share our awareness of vulnerability—vulnerability is part of the human condition. In a right relationship, where justice is primary, acceptance of the stranger (in and among us) is a given. Accepting one another, as our Unitarian Universalist principle states, means relating to one another as we are, not as we think another ought to be.

The search committee took Ron out to dinner, then back to the chairperson's lovely house overlooking a lake with a pool in the deck.

Following dessert, a couple hours of interviewing took place. At 10:30 p.m., the host announced it was pool time. Ron said that he had not brought along swim trunks, but if he could borrow a pair, he'd be right in. Imagine his surprise and feelings when he appeared pool side as the only one of the ten who wasn't naked. He was embarrassed, chagrined, and angry for being put in such an awkward position.

The thoughtlessness of the search committee had turned an already apprehensive evening into a dread-filled one for Ron. Humiliated and feeling vulnerable, Ron wanted nothing more to do with this congregation. This context and others heighten our awareness of the need to protect the vulnerable, the "stranger," in any church relationship and to make just relations a priority.

Twenty years ago, I attended my first General Assembly as a parish minister. My wife and I were staying in one of the dorms that was isolated from the rest of the campus. One afternoon, a respected and admired senior colleague asked if he could borrow our room for the evening—he had developed a special relationship with a woman and since their spouses were also at the Assembly, they needed a safe, private place. The woman was the wife of a close friend whom we all knew; in fact, the senior colleague had been her husband's mentor.

Young and naive, not wanting to disappoint, yet sensing that this was not right, feeling pressured by a senior colleague who told us we were doing him a favor, my wife and I talked and talked that afternoon trying to reach an arrangement that would alleviate our anxiety and take care of everyone's needs. Most of all, we wanted the problem to just go away.

I get angry when I recall this incident, now several decades old. The vulnerability my wife and I felt, the loneliness of being new, inexperienced, and unable to tell anyone about the pressure and anxiety, all contributed to a situation that should never have existed, a context that was not right, a relationship that was unbalanced and unfair, a relation that was unjust.

"For you [too] were strangers. . . ." We all know how it feels to be vulnerable. And we know how it feels when our vulnerability is acknowledged, accepted, and protected: It makes us feel listened to, respected, safe, and affirmed, all important to a just relationship. These take on additional meanings in a context that involves a church's children: creating a congregational environment that is just for children is as important as it is for adults. Many congregations are recognizing the glaring need to make right relations a guiding principle in religious education programs. Making sure that a child is never left alone with an adult, having windows in classroom doors, having immediate access to a phone (for emergencies), making sure that all teachers and child-care providers are clear about goals and expectations, and having an abuse/misconduct policy are some congregational steps needed for just relationships.

The conditions and opportunities for protecting the vulnerable and accepting one another are many. Just relations demand that we remain accepting of each other, protecting the stranger.

5. Restitution

Principle: Respect for the interdependent web of all existence of which we are a part.

(Ecclesiastes 3:1-13)

With a grand, almost cosmic view, the writer of Ecclesiastes (3:1-13) spins the popular verses that remind us that all of life is giving and receiving, changing, always in movement. A hymn affirms this wisdom: "It is right, it should be so: we were made for joy and woe; and when this we rightly know, safely through the world we go." An unexpected balancing takes place in this give and take.

Similarly, relationships go through cycles, ups and downs: They may be carefree and intense, one-sided, co-equal, and interdependent. Yet ultimately, if a relationship is not balanced and fair, it is not just or right. In an unbalanced relationship, an unjust one, there is the need for renewal: Renewing a right relation is never easy, often strenuous, upsetting for many. But balance must be restored if justice is a priority.

Samuel's wife Phyllis was embarrassed and humiliated by his stalking and subsequent imprisonment: She was confused and desperate; she felt isolated. Samuel had thrown the church community out of balance, and Phyllis thought her relationship with the congregation had been damaged beyond repair. Only after lots of attention and lengthy conversations, invitations, and encouragement to attend church functions did a renewing of right relations occur between Phyllis and the church.

The Unitarian Universalist Principles speak of "respect for the interdependent web of all existence of which we are a part." When we understand and feel our interdependence, the push and pull of life's balancing act, when we finally know that we are in this (life) together, then the inevitable restitution that must come in a just relation can be made possible, even in the face of almost overwhelming odds.

Marie Fortune tells the story of a young woman whose nightmare of physical and verbal abuse finally ended with her father's death. When the family found out, everyone was shocked, but wondered what they could do since he was dead. Her uncle (her father's brother) set restitution in motion. He flew to see her and apologized for his brother: He was ashamed of what he had done. Her uncle wanted her to know that he would do whatever it took to set things right, to begin restoring balance in her life: financial support, therapy, whatever.

While most of the woman's renewing would have to be worked through alone, her uncle's show of support was a meaningful contribution to balancing a relationship that had been an unjust one for years.

We cannot underestimate the value of renewing a right relationship. Unjust relations vary, but members of a congregation must examine thoroughly what role they might play in restoring balance and justice, making whole what has been broken. Our desire to "affirm and promote respect for the interdependent web of all existence" is served and strengthened by nothing less.

6. Vindication

Principle: The goal of world community with peace, liberty, and justice for all.

(Ezekiel 18:25-32; Luke 18:1-8)

"Turn, then, and live," Ezekiel (18:32) implores his listeners. Living means relationships. In the congregational setting, turning away from an unjust relation to seek a right one may mean removing those barriers or setting free the layers of hurt created by imbalance. Vindication (from the Latin, meaning "to set free") can restore and renew balance and promote living; then the goal of "justice for all" can be made real.

In the religious community, we can't be expected to unpack every wrong or hurt: To balance every injustice in a wrong relationship would be an admirable but exhausting and unrealistic goal. Some members have suffered injustice outside of the church; a few may decide to share an emotional or social wrong they have experienced, while others may never say a word. A congregation's pastoral and governing leadership may decide, when appropriate, to converse with a member about restitution and vindication—what they seek, what might make living whole, what they need "to turn and live."

When an unjust relation has been committed in the church context, the congregation can and must play a larger role. Turning and moving on might be accomplished by a conversation or apology, a recognition or thank you, a correction or reimbursement: There are probably dozens of ways to make right the myriad of wrongs that can occur in a congregation. This is simply to recognize that an unjust relation will involve some layering of imbalance and hurt that must be removed for vindication to occur.

Vindication is not always smooth. How the events, the people, and the way the other five elements and principles have been addressed will determine the result. In this sense, vindication does not stand alone: It is the result of a process whose goal is just relations.

7. Accountability

Principle: The right of conscience and the use of the democratic process within our congregations.

(II Timothy 1:7)

When Russell began abusing his congregational relationship as a way to harass Krista, Kurt was quick to decide that the church leadership had to take a stand—it was not his, a committee's, or someone else's issue to respond to. He also admitted: "If it's happening now, it will happen again."

Kurt's reaction was quick, timely, and firm. Unfortunately, too many congregations don't respond to unjust relationships until it is too late. Our institutions and members are susceptible to abuse, misdirection, and pressure tactics from individuals or groups. Right relationships mean having an institutional process and context to which individuals are responsible and accountable, and having someone to keep an objective overview of the institution and monitor activity. Kurt was aware of the situation because of his involvement with Krista and Russell. The congregation's board finally had to be made aware of and respond to the circumstances because of the injustice taking place. They also needed guidance, a policy, and process to follow.

In another example, Ric was a long-term member of the congregation. He had participated on every committee and served on nearly every board. It wasn't unusual for Ric to hold several positions at the same time. He lived close to the church, so he made it a habit to stop in for lunch, perform repairs, let people in (he had a key). The congregation wasn't sure what they would do without Ric—he was everything to everybody.

Imagine the board chair's surprise and shock when she received a letter from the new minister of religious education, Sylvia, accusing Ric of harassment. Crude jokes, sexually suggestive comments, inappropriate visits, and stalking were just a few of the accusations she made in her lengthy letter that cited dates, times, examples, and possible witnesses.

When Ric heard about Sylvia's letter he was outraged and defensive. He accused Sylvia of emotional instability, professional incompetence, and blackmail. With both letters in hand, the congregation's leadership listened to each person and remained perplexed—they had no idea about what to do.

As suggested by the Unitarian Universalist Association, Molly, an area minister, was asked to listen to Sylvia and Ric and make suggestions to an investigating team that had been appointed by the board's executive committee. While Molly found breaches of a just relationship, questionable behaviors and practices by both Ric and Sylvia, what was stunning was the degree to which the institution had colluded—unknowingly supported—the destructive and divisive relationship that was now well known and talked about beyond the leadership circle.

As Paul suggests in II Timothy (1:7), the leadership of a congregation has the discipline, resources, and ability to create a climate of just relations. Our societies are based in congregational polity—they establish their own guidelines and policies using "the right of conscience and the use of the democratic process" as an ideal. . . . Growing consideration is being given to structures that enhance the opportunities for right relations in congregations—policies, guidelines, or covenants that make clear what is expected from members as they relate with one another since only the congregation can govern itself.

Elie Wiesel writes, "The meaning of life is to be found in every encounter." We live in a time of heightened sensationalism: The limits of what we expect, believe, and experience are tested and broadened daily. Religious societies have not escaped being cast in a role in this drama. Unitarian Universalist congregations can claim no innocence: The injustices that have occurred have been devastating to our congregational life— we have read about the growing numbers of those who have been wronged by unjust relations. Some have experienced the injustice first hand.

Yet our desire and hope for right relations continues. Our congregations are growing; our church schools are booming; our Association supports us as we explore what it means to be spiritually, culturally, and politically diverse. In this context, desire for just relations is paramount. We have as our guides the collected experiences and wisdom of the years. Together they form a broad base from which to discuss and explore, respond to, and create policy, to practice just relations in a safe congregation.

Accountability Grid

Activity	Ministerial Fellowship Committee (UUA board-appointed standing committee)	UUA Department of Ministry	UU Ministers Association
Support for ministers and students	None	Personal, professional, and financial counseling; conflict resolution	Meetings and retreats, Good Offices persons, grievance procedures
Teaching of ministers and students	Mentorships, career assessment	Career counseling, mentorships	Mentorships, professional resources, CENTER programs
Credentialing ministers	Admission to, review of, and removal from Fellowship	Staff support and counsel	Appoints two members to MFC
Sets standards for ministers	UUA bylaws, MFC rules and policies	Staff support and counsel	*Guidelines, Code of Professional Practice*, UUMA bylaws
Disciplining of ministers and students	Responds to formal complaints against ministers; informed by UUMA *Guidelines* and *Code*; governed by UUA bylaws, MFC rules and policies	Counsels, negotiates, offers pastoral response; in case of students, may initiate removal of candidate status	*UUMA Guidelines, Code*, bylaws; responds to grievances against members
Relating to congregations	Serves congregations	Serves the congregations, ministers, and students	No direct relationship
Relating to students	Career assessment, credentialing	Provides financial aid, assists with internships, counseling	Membership, collegiality
Disciplining congregations or members	None	Consulting	None

Just Relations Grid

Justice-Making Element (Marie Fortune, *Is Nothing Sacred*)	UU Principle	Biblical Reference
Acknowledging: a person feels heard and affirmed in their worth.	The inherent worth and dignity of every person	I Corinthians 3:16; each of us is sacred.
Compassion: "suffering" with a person	Justice, equity, and compassion in human relations	Luke 4:18; compassion and justice for the broken and disenfranchised
Truth-telling: looking at all of a person's circumstances, all dimensions	A free and responsible search for truth and meaning	Daniel 13:1-63 (or Susanna 1-63); be steadfast in pursuing the truth
Protecting: accepting what has occurred and taking action	Acceptance of one another	Deuteronomy 10:19; giving shelter to the vulnerable
Restitution: renewing right relations, patching the broken wholeness	Respect for the inderdependent web of all existence of which we are a part	Ecclesiastes 3:1-13; a connectedness to life that can't be broken, an interdependent wholeness
Vindication: setting free, making things right	The goal of world community with peace, liberty, and justice for all.	Ezekiel 18:25-32, Luke 18:1-8; turning to life
Accountability: there is an institutional process and responsibility	The right of conscience and the use of the democratic process within our congregations.	II Timothy 1:7; we have the means to make relations right

6   The Courage to Heal

Goals
- To explore the element of healing in defining right relations and safe spaces
- To gain understanding of attitudes and activities that promote healing
- To gain understanding of concept and processes of forgiveness, reconciliation, and acceptance.

Materials
- One copy of the discussion essay for each participant
- One copy of Resource 11 for each participant
- Copies of *Singing the Living Tradition*
- Chalice or candle and matches

Preparation
- Distribute the discussion essay to each participant with instructions to read it before the session begins.
- Read the discussion essay by Michelle Hunt before the group meets.
- From the discussion essay, write each "attitude that promotes healing" on individual slips of paper and on newsprint.

Session Plan

Gathering and Centering   5 minutes

Light the chalice and read these opening words by Donna DiSciullo from "Re-weaving the Threads, A Movement Toward Wholeness":

> Come Sacred Spirit, come
> breathe your invigorating and
>   enlivening passion through us
>   as we covenant to keep this space
>   holy
>   healthy
>   healing.

Focusing 30 minutes

Summarize the goals for this session.

If this is the first gathering of this group for Creating Safe Congregation work, establish group guidelines. Refer to page 10 for the procedure.

Engage participants in a discussion of the church as a safe place. Say something like "As Unitarian Universalists, we affirm that the religious community is a locus of the sacred, a place where we strive to live in the vision of justice, equity, and compassion in our relationships and encourage each other to spiritual growth.

"Implicit in the vision and a prerequisite for spiritual growth is trust, so we can open ourselves, let down our protective armor. It is in the risk of vulnerability that we have the possibility of encountering the sacred in ourselves and others.

"Our human experience leads us to develop and use a variety of strategies that protect us from hurt. These strategies become layers of protection that keep us from feeling vulnerable. Spiritual growth and personal growth can be stifled by these layers of protection. As important as the work is, in spite of our yearning to know that which connects us with the truth about who we are, we hesitate and avoid the work. We find it much easier to do the rational work, the empirical study, the logical debate—even at church. But in our religious community, the miraculous possibility exists that we can feel safe enough and trust enough that we are able to work through the protective layers and risk opening up. One of the most noble functions of our religious communities is providing a safe place that promotes the possibility of transformation."

Discuss the following questions in a whole group or in small groups that report back to the whole group.

- What characteristics make a church feel safe?
- Do you feel safe at church? Why? What supports or undermines your feeling of safety?
- Is this issue important for you?
- Is this an important characteristic of a healthy church?
- How do members of a church relate to each other in ways that contribute to a feeling of safety?
- What aspects of spiritual growth does safety make possible?

As an activity for internalizing "attitudes that promote healing," hand out the slips of paper you prepared. Ask members of the group to read and comment on them if they wish. Solicit suggestions for other helpful attitudes from the group.

Reflecting 20 minutes

Refer participants to the section "Dimensions of Congregational Healing" in the discussion essay. Explain each wedge of the circle, especially the difference between Anger I (focused and blaming) and Anger II (diffused and generalized). Read and emphasize the Three Rules.

Distribute Resource 11. Using this diagram, ask participants to reflect on their own responses to an experience of abuse—clergy, child, congregant—known to their congregation. Allow five minutes of individual reflection time.

Invite responses from participants. Remind them of their group guidelines or Covenant for Openness and Sharing. Are there similarities in responses? Differences? Ask them what they noticed in their sharing or what conclusions they could draw from their exchange.

Exploring   30 minutes

Engage the participants in a discussion of forgiveness.

For some people, forgiveness is the way to heal. For others, particularly people who have been victims of abuse, the expectation that they should forgive is a burden that has no bearing on their potential to heal. However, forgiveness is an important idea related to healing. The following meditation, "Forgiveness," is by Sara Moores Campbell. Read aloud this meditation and use it as the basis for a discussion of forgiveness.

> There is incredible power in forgiveness. But forgiveness is not rational. One can seldom find a reason to forgive/to be forgiven. Forgiveness is often undeserved. It may require a dimension of justice (penance, in traditional terms), but not always, for what it holds sacred is not fairness, but self-respect and community. Forgiveness does not wipe away guilt, but invites reconciliation. And it is as important to be able to forgive as it is to be forgiven.
>
> No, we do not forgive and forget. But when we invite the power of forgiveness, we release ourselves from some of the destructive hold the past has on us. Our hatred, our anger, our need to feel wronged—those will destroy us, whether a relationship is reconciled or not.
>
> But we cannot just will ourselves to enter into forgiveness, either as givers or receivers. We can know it is right and that we want to do it and still not be able to.
>
> We can, however, be open and receptive to the power of forgiveness, which, like any gift of the spirit, isn't our own making. Its power is rooted in love. The Greek word for this kind of love is *agape*. Martin Luther King, Jr., defined *agape* as "Love seeking to preserve and create community." This kind of love is human, but it is also the grace of a transcendent power that lifts us out of ourselves. It transforms and heals; and even when we are separated by time or space or death, it reconciles us to ourselves and to life. For its power abides not just between us but within us. If we invited the power of *agape* to heal our personal wounds and give us the gift of forgiveness, we would give our world a better chance of survival.

Ask participants to speak from experience in defining "forgiveness," "*agape*," "reconciliation," and "compassion." Include all participants in the discussion.

Integrating   20 minutes

Refer participants to the section "Symptoms of a Congregation Experiencing Trauma or Loss" in the discussion essay. Engage the participants in a discussion of attitudes that promote healing, referring to the diagram.

Show the group the list of attitudes you printed on newsprint. Ask participants to read and comment on them. Solicit suggestions for other helpful attitudes from the group.

Invite suggestions for additional activities and ways people can minister to each other at this time in the congregation.

Closing   15 minutes

Invite the participants to participate in the following ritual.

Say, "Spirit of Community, in which we share and find strength, and common purpose, we turn our minds and hearts toward one another seeking to bring into our circle of concern all who need our love and support: those who are ill, those who are in pain, either in body or in spirit, those who are lonely, those who have been wronged."

(*From where they sit, people may say the names of those to be remembered, or light a candle, or tie a ribbon on a tree represented by a large branch.*)

Continue, "We are part of a web of life that makes us one with all humanity, one with all the universe. We are grateful for the miracle of consciousness that we share, the consciousness that gives us the power to remember, to love, to care."

Close with these words by Donna DiSciullo from "Re-Weaving the Threads, A Movement Toward Wholeness":

For those among us who have experienced abuse
    —we are truly sorry
For those among us who have inflicted abuse
    —may new learning and grace redeem us
For those of us who have stood by in silence
    —give us the courage of our voice
From this day forward may we be creators of safe and sacred space.

Evaluation and Planning

Consider the following questions. Reflect on them and discuss them with your co-leader(s).

1. How do I feel about this session now?
2. What was good or not so good about this session? Why?
3. If I were to lead this session again, what would I do differently?
4. What preparations do I need to make for the next session?

Healing in Right Relations
Michelle Hunt

As president of my church board, it was my responsibility to inform the congregation of complaints detailing sexual misconduct by our former minister. Try to understand the intensity and variety of emotions this triggered. The stress on the community—a community that took great pride in its warm and welcoming ways—was intense. For some people and victims, the trauma was soul wounding—the pain so intense that their belief system and trust in the church was severely shaken.

Loyalties were divided; people were outraged at the former minister; people were outraged because the new minister and I were not sympathetic toward the former minister; others struggled with the reminder of past abuse; and others just didn't want to hear anything about it. We lost some members, which added to the pain. Casual remarks from good people who did not understand caused more hurt. Individually and collectively, we had much to learn and much to heal.

We survived. This is a growing, dynamic, and healthy congregation. A new sanctuary and religious education wing that more than doubled the size of our church building provides tangible evidence of healing. However, the more subtle and important evidence of our healing is found in our understanding and articulation of the qualities that make our religious community a safe place. As a community, we take pride in our integrity. We have great clarity about the sacred potential of our religious community and we are intentional about fulfilling that potential.

This essay reflects our struggle, our learnings, our healing. In "Reflections Toward a Unitarian Universalist Theological Understanding of Clergy Sexual Abuse," Thomas Mikelson writes, "The work of the religious community is to create and preserve the safety and trust in which spiritual growth can occur. . . . The fact that we gather in communities of faith suggests, beyond our hunger for spiritual growth, a need for the safety that allows us to let down defenses which usually stand in the way of self-examination. We can allow ourselves to be vulnerable only when we are reasonably confident that others in our communities will not take advantage of our vulnerability."

The religious community has the profound potential to encourage and support spiritual growth. This potential is fulfilled only when the community is healthy and whole—when members of the community feel safe and trust that they will be accepted and valued. We hope that all religious communities would always offer safety. However, many circumstances in the life of a congregation might jeopardize the sense of being in a safe place. How we respond to the circumstances and how we relate to each other—even when there is stress, distress, loss, or hurt—is critical to the well-being of the community and to an individual's potential to grow within the community. Loss of that potential is a terrible human loss. When faith in the religious community is shaken for any reason, we must find the courage, determination, and wisdom to heal.

An Invitation to Heal
"The healing that arises within us has its own timing. And we need not push and we need not rush because it will come when it is ready."
—Wayne Muller, *Touching the Divine*

We can neither prescribe nor dictate that healing happen. We can only invite healing to happen. And we invite healing to happen through an open response, justice-making, specific attitudes, and specific activities. Healing ourselves requires us to do the uncomfortable work of identifying the emotions we are experiencing so that we can move beyond the stage where our emotions control. Then we can find our way back to comfort within the community. This can be a rocky journey, but it is a journey we must take to be where we want to be—in right relations with the religious community. Healing personal hurt and organizational hurt is possible—be hopeful and remember that it will happen in its own time. Members of congregations who experience trauma such as ministerial sexual misconduct will react in different ways to the incident. In addition, individuals may experience reactions at different times and in a different sequence. To understand this better, refer to the following.

Dimensions of Congregational Healing
The symptoms of a congregation experiencing trauma and loss can be reviewed on the graphic below. For congregations, healing means mov-

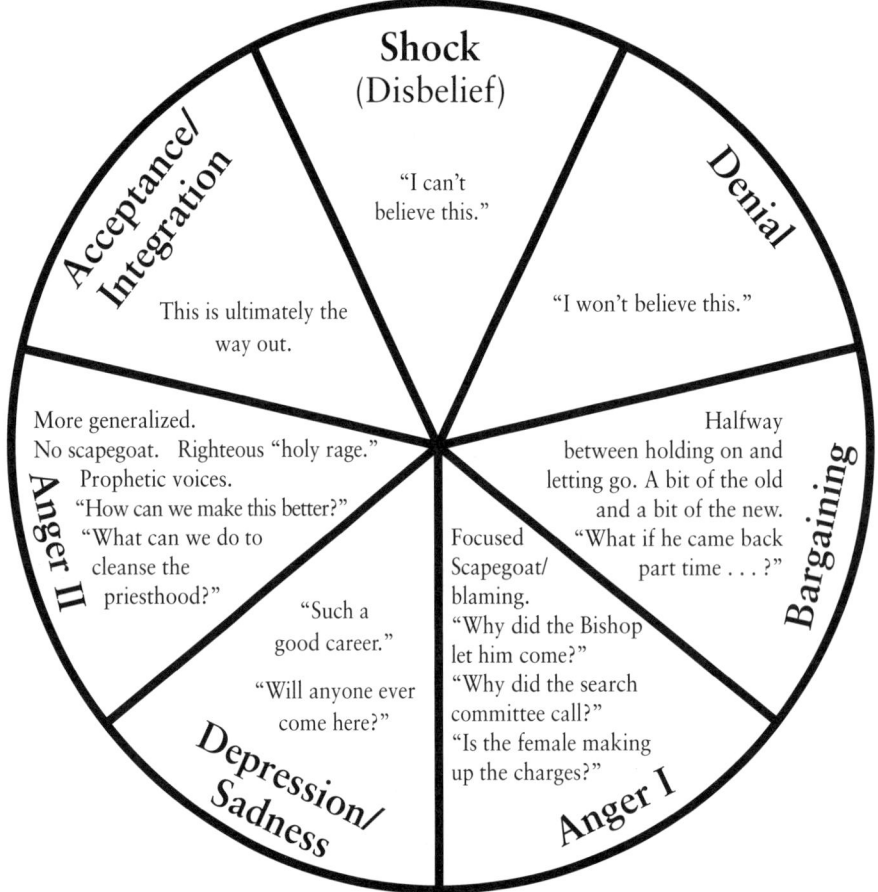

ing through hurt feelings toward acceptance and reconciliation with the experience. The experience and the lessons learned should be integrated into the community's story. There is hope, energy, and enthusiasm for what the church can accomplish as a religious community. When there is openness, respect, and honesty, the community feels safe.

Three Rules
1. People can enter at any point.
2. People can go clockwise, counter clockwise, or jump across again and again.
3. This circle tells people that no matter how different they feel, they are a unity.

—from "Trauma Debriefing: Congregational Model."
Copyright ©1991 by Chilton R. Knudsen. All rights reserved.

Symptoms of a Congregation Experiencing Trauma or Loss
After a traumatic event, a congregation goes through some predictable phases during the process of moving from discovery to recovery. A chaotic period of pain, distrust, and anger surfaces after the secret is exposed. There may be relief from facing the truth, yet the overwhelming seriousness of the problem and the victimization within the congregation tends to polarize members. It's important to name and express feelings through congregational forums and meetings in order to move on to recovery and resolution. This diagram illustrates some symptoms of a congregation in the discovery-chaos phase.

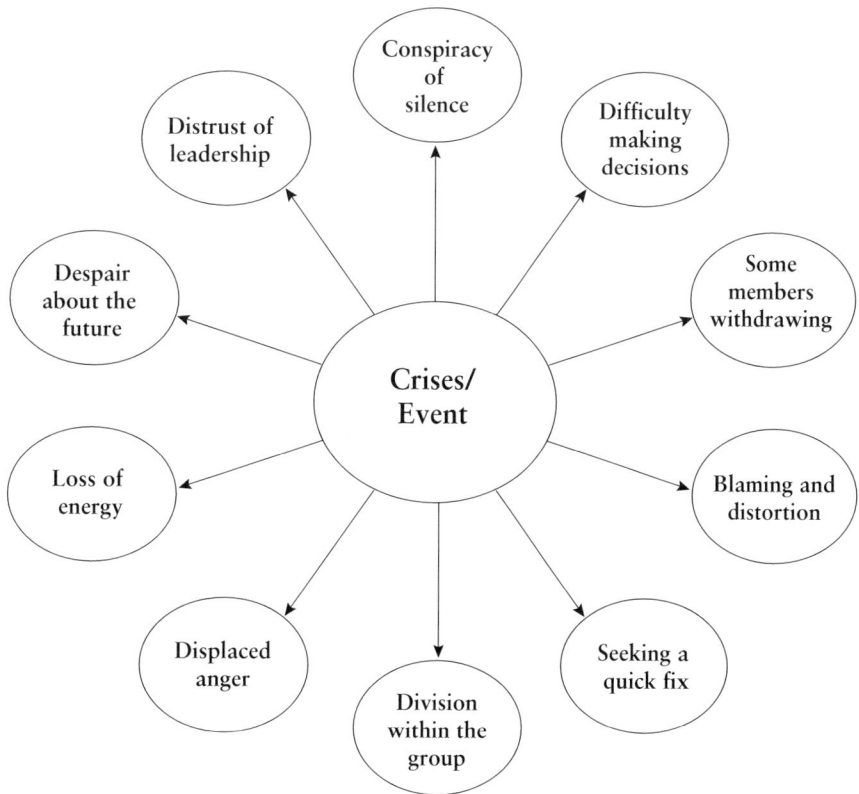

(Based on symptoms of post-traumatic stress syndrome as identified in Chilton Knudsen's research adapted for the study of congregations.)

Minimize Hurt Through Authentic and Appropriate Communication

"And the organization itself, if told the truth and assisted in processing its pain, can emerge with greater integrity, justice, and self-respect."
—David R. Brubaker, conflict consultant and mediator

Minimizing hurt does not mean silence or secrecy about the event. Keeping secrets even for the right reasons does not work. Information that includes some detail and explains the consequences makes denial harder. Respect and maintain confidentiality, but keep the congregation informed. When there is a lack of accurate information, misinformation will likely fill the void.

When the incident or situation is serious and emotions are high, congregations should find a trained person from outside the congregation to facilitate large and small group discussion. A conflict mediator would be ideal. At the least you will need an impartial discussion facilitator who can create a safe space for people to express their feelings and have those feelings validated. The district executive is a good person to contact for human resources.

Conveying bad news is difficult. Express the facts without judgment. For example, "A member of this congregation has told the board president that a trustee has been making sexually harassing telephone calls. The allegation has been taken very seriously. In consultation with our district executive, the board of trustees has agreed to organize an investigation that we expect to take two weeks. You will be informed as to the disposition."

In summary, the congregation needs accurate, timely information. An outside, trained person from the Unitarian Universalist Association or district field staff or a community action organization is needed to provide a safe space for the congregation to process what has happened. Processing takes time; people will be at different stages of understanding and integration at various times. When the trauma is caused by sexual abuse or misconduct, there should be scheduled periodic opportunities to talk in a safe environment for two years—maybe longer. In the case where an allegation is false, the consultant can still help the congregation understand and integrate the experience.

Minimizing Hurt Through Intervention

We are sealed in.
The only way out is through
fire, and I do not want a single
hair of a single head singed.
—Sharon Olds, from "Late"

Avoid the tragedy of additional hurt or wounding through appropriate intervention. If there is an allegation or suspicion of sexual exploitation of minors or the abuse or neglect of children, make a report immediately to the police or local child protective agency. There is no alternative. We have an ethical mandate to protect the children.

If there is an allegation of sexual misconduct or harassment about the minister, church staff, or leadership, take steps immediately to avoid additional victimization. Do not give in to the temptation to deny. History shows that in the vast majority of allegations, the victim is telling the truth. Early intervention is difficult, but we must do everything that we can to create a safe place for the victim/accuser, the accused, and everyone else in the community. Prevention of additional hurt logically makes healing easier.

Procedures for counseling, support, and reporting include: Listening as the person tells the story. Believing the story. Affirming the act of telling. Being honest in your response. Taking notes on disclosure conversation. Reporting disclosure to the congregation president, minister, or religious educator as agreed upon by your congregational process, as well as child protection services or department of social services, if a child is disclosing. Referring the perpetrator, victim, and families to professional services. Seeking support services and pastoral counseling for the congregation.

Attitudes That Promote Healing

What can one person do? Make a personal commitment to promote healing. You have many personal attitudes and qualities that will invite and promote healing on both the corporate and individual levels.

- Offer hope. As Norman Cousins says, "Hope puts the spirit to work."
- Find the personal courage to explore the possibility that you may at times cause hurt to others.
- Be a good listener. Be present to the other person. The listener may not need answers as much as listening.
- Be patient. People process feelings and heal on different schedules.
- Stick to the facts. Discourage rumor. Respect confidentiality.
- Affirm the pain or hurt of others. "I am sorry this happened to you." "You did nothing to deserve this." "Of course you feel hurt."
- Support justice making. True remorse and restitution are keys to justice making.
- Screen your actions and statements through the filter of two questions, "Will this help to heal?" and "How will this affect those who are hurt?" Responsible people respond to their feelings without causing pain or hurt to others.
- Minister to each other!

Prevention, Education, and Healing

When there is tragedy or loss, we always ask, "Why?" When there is no answer and no possibility of justice, what can we do to promote healing? Often there is comfort in working toward prevention. Developing strategies for prevention is a sure way to give power to individuals and the congregation.

At the core of prevention is a set of clear, well-known policies and procedures. Procedures include the process for reporting sexual misconduct and sexual harassment to the community and reporting child abuse or neglect to the appropriate authorities. If the problem can be handled within the community (mishandling of funds, sexual harassment that involves adult members), it is better if the congregation has already created guidelines for investigation, judicature, and possible action. Sample policies are available from the UUA Department of Religious Education *Safety/Abuse Clearing House packet* and should be used as a guide to developing your church's policies. The process of developing policies will increase awareness of the issues.

Ongoing education about the nature of the congregation and ministry is solid prevention for much inappropriate behavior. When the congregation can easily identify its healthy characteristics, it more easily recognizes unhealthy or inappropriate behavior. There is the possibility of earlier, preventive intervention. Include teaching and discussing the grieving process. Loss on any level will be more easily understood. This discussion is valuable for the individual and encourages an appropriate institutional response.

Be intentional about supporting and financing education for lay leaders. This education may include activities such as going to General Assembly and district meetings, attending leadership training, and attending Unitarian Universalist Association sponsored conferences. Lay leaders and responsible members of congregations need to understand ministry, be aware of the dynamics of congregational life and the denomination, and learn how to support and maintain healthy ministries and safe congregations.

Conflict is inevitable and even healthy, but unresolved conflict festers and becomes toxic. Because Unitarian Universalist congregations operate on democratic principles, compromise and consensus are methods used for decision making. Specific skills promote conflict resolution and reaching consensus. Learn the principles. You do not have to be an expert to understand and use the basics.

Justice Making and Healing
"There can be no healing without justice and justice requires courage."
—Marie Fortune, *Clergy Misconduct*

Justice making is a necessary element in the healing process. (See Session 5 for more discussion of justice making.)

Healing Services and Rituals
Services and rituals that focus on healing can be powerful vehicles for promoting healing for individuals and congregations. They give everyone the opportunity to recognize that although they may react differently to the same circumstance, they are united in their concern. A ritual is included in Session 4. Other materials for healing services are available from the Department of Religious Education.

Integration, Forgiveness, Reconciliation, and Acceptance

"[Integration is] the only appropriate response that is available, productive, practical, and growthful."

—Celia Hahn, *Sexual Paradox*

We need to consider the concepts of forgiveness and reconciliation and how they relate to healing. The meaning of forgiveness is different for different people. The advice to "forgive and forget" may be helpful, but it can be used to avoid a more thorough process of acceptance and reconciliation. Victims of abuse or other trauma should not and need not be encouraged to "forgive and forget"—at least not in the context of saying that what a perpetrator did was okay or does not matter. "Letting go" has become a cliché, but the concept may be more helpful. Following is a reading on the subject of forgiveness by the Reverend Sara Campbell. Individuals and institutions need to integrate even painful experiences into their story. An authentic process for healing can be a good source of self-respect that gives a positive aspect to the story. Balance the painful or hurtful story with celebration of the strengths of the person or community. Justice and restitution also contribute much to reconciliation and acceptance.

"The whole point of getting in touch with your spirituality is to enhance your healing, not to escape it. Spirituality is not a shortcut through any stage of the healing process. It's not an alternative to feeling your anger, to working through the pain, to fully acknowledging the damage done. Rather it should be an enrichment to healing, a source from which you can draw comfort and inspiration."—Ellen Bass and Laura Davis, *The Courage to Heal: A Comprehensive Guide to Healing from Child Sexual Abuse*

The Courage to Heal

You will know that healing has taken place when you see evidence of integration, reconciliation with experience (not necessarily with the perpetrator or an adversary), and acceptance. It may be months or years before this happens. Be hopeful. Keep the vision of the community restored to wholeness as a clear goal. Be kind and patient with your own progress and the progress of others. Be courageous in terms of facing what needs to be done to invite healing. Our faith communities and the potential they offer are worthy of our best efforts.

Dimensions of Congregational Healing

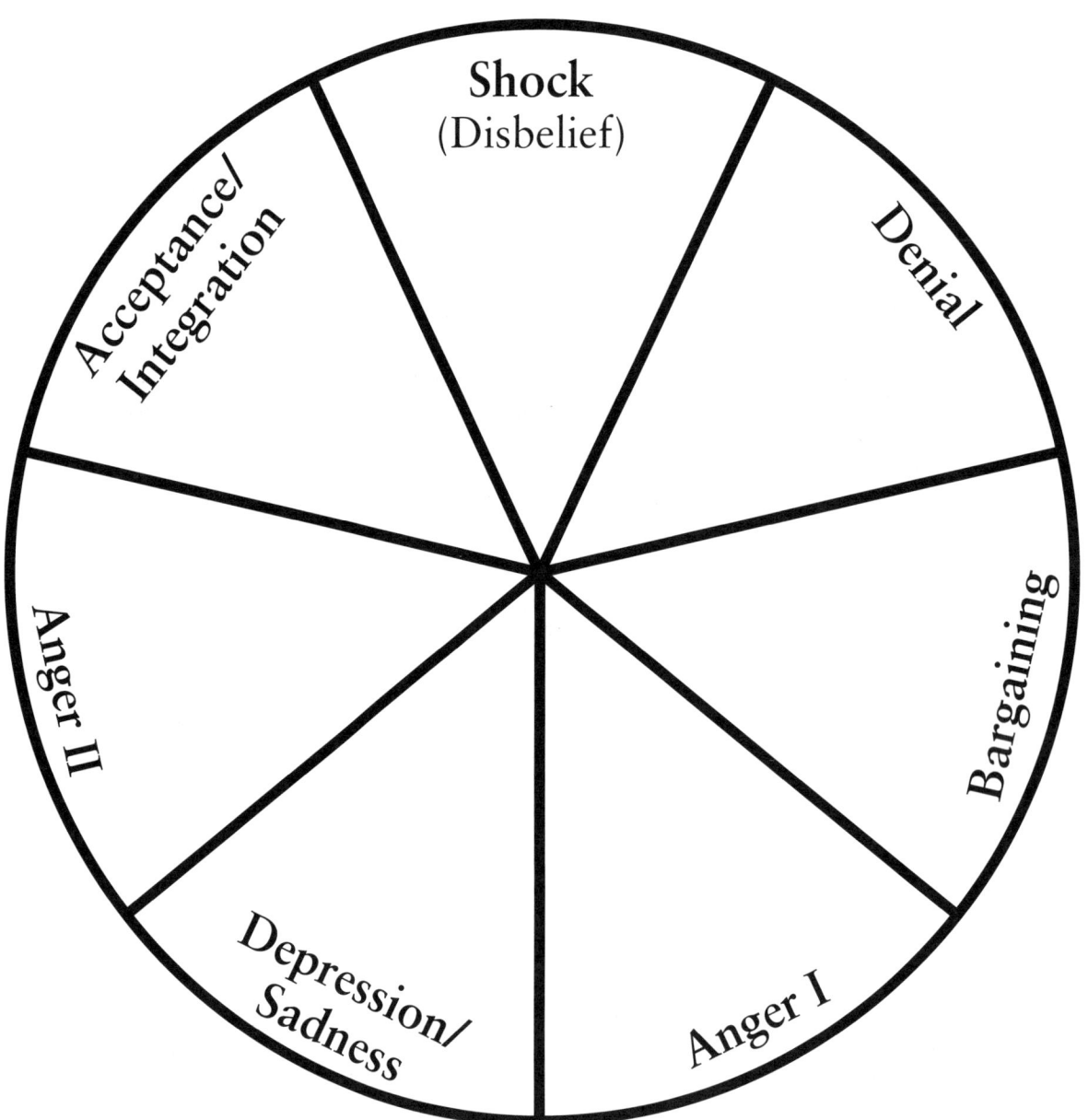

3 Rules

1. People can enter at any point.
2. People can go clockwise, counter clockwise, or can jump across, again and again.
3. This circle tells people that no matter now different they look and feel, they are a unity.

Reprinted with permission.

7 Creating and Reviewing Our Covenant

As awareness about abusive relationships in our congregations has grown, the Unitarian Universalist Association has been challenged to offer a response that will help prevent sexual abuse by ministers and in our congregations generally. Each UUMA chapter group has offered training to raise awareness of these issues. District-based teams (Safe Congregation Teams) were created and trained in most districts. Almost all Unitarian Universalist Association field staff received training on this issue.

Beyond these steps to raise awareness and provide resources to deal with clergy misconduct, we felt called to make our congregations safe spaces where people would be able to open themselves to the possibility of transformation and greater spiritual depth without fear of violation by their minister or others in positions of institutional power in the congregation.

However, we soon came to the realization that "safety" was something that no congregation could legislate, even with the best of intentions. Even if it were possible to guarantee safety, the real issue is an understanding of what it means to be in "right relationship." Our understanding of the task moved from the provision of "safety," protection from violation, to the need to move toward positive, healthy, right relationships within our congregations. Clergy misconduct and sexual abuse are clearly violations of "right relationship." But our task is broader.

A focus on misconduct and abuse could have led us to concentrate on the issues of policy, notification of authorities, and legal and liability questions. These, of course, are important and are addressed in this program with references to appropriate resources. But by understanding our task as the creation of right relations in our congregations, we opened ourselves to reflect on ethical and theological grounding, and therefore our reasonable expectations, for personal and institutional relationships within our worshiping communities.

Our concerns centered around what persons, all persons, in congregations should reasonably be able to expect of one another . . . what we can honestly promise one another about our life together in religious community. This is the language of covenant.

A Covenant Process

Unitarian Universalist congregations and the Unitarian Universalist Association of Congregations are united by a covenant. The covenanting process is founded on the principle of freedom and a commitment of mutuality. We covenant—our free and voluntary pledge of mutuality—to affirm and promote the dignity of every person, the importance of personal responsibility, and the basic interdependence of all people. We promise to one another "our mutual trust and support." Our covenanting takes place among the congregations of the Association and within each congregation.

> "A covenant refers to the promises or commitments that people make to each other in the context of religious community."
> —Chulak and Morgan, "Mission-Covenant," *Growing: A Congregational Enhancement Series for Unitarian Universalists*

> "All churches have covenants with their . . . members. They are well defined or ill defined, written or unwritten, official or unofficial, openly agreed upon or unmentioned or assumed. It is not a choice of whether there will be a covenant . . . rather it is a choice as to the kind of covenant they will have."—Brown, "Church Staff Teams That Win," *Growing: A Congregational Enhancement Series for Unitarian Universalists*

> "A covenant statement gives expression to your identity, in particular the qualities that will sustain you in your life together and the 'promise' you make to each other in religious community. Covenant is the commitment you make to each other. It is your response to the question: 'What are the qualities we want in our life and work together?'"—*Congregational Handbook*

Many congregations and other Unitarian Universalist communities have engaged in a vision/mission/covenant process in recent years. If yours has not done so, or if you engaged in this process some time ago, we encourage you to enter into a full vision/mission/covenant process. (See *Congregational Handbook*, Section 1.)

This process begins with the development of a shared vision, an articulation of what the community ultimately wants to create as a congregation. To move from having a vision to implementing that vision you need to clarify your mission. A covenant is an articulation of the values and qualities that a congregation wants to promote to enhance and support its members in living out its mission.

If you have completed this process recently, your congregational mission and covenant statements may form the starting point for this process. For example:

As a welcoming and accepting, diverse and inquiring religious community, we unite to provide an environment which stimulates a free exchange and exploration of ideas, fosters spiritual and intellectual growth, and serves as a base for active outreach to benefit the world around us.—Unitarian Universalist Church of Corpus Christi, Texas

The Dublin Unitarian Universalist Church is a sharing, nurturing, and caring community which promotes spiritual growth and development along with intellectual freedom. We provide an atmosphere of acceptance of one another while seeking to understand ourselves and our universe. We foster an ethical basis for living and celebrate in life's diversity. We reaffirm our respect for others which empowers us to act on our beliefs to improve our community and relieve social injustice.—Dublin Unitarian Universalist Church, Dublin, OH

The *Congregational Handbook* (available from your district office) includes an excellent section on mission covenant and suggests processes to follow. The Department of Congregational, District, and Extension Services also offers a more detailed piece on this subject.

To covenant as a congregation to move toward "right relations and safe spaces" recognizes the importance of safety as a prerequisite for personal transformation and growth. We ask you to focus on what makes, or could make, your community one that its members experience as safe. Thus we focus on the elements of mission that call us to right relations within the congregation, recognizing that to the extent we can embody such right relationships they become the gift we can offer, not only to ourselves, but to the world around us.

This is emphatically not a process only for those congregations that have experienced clergy misconduct or abuse of other kinds. We see this process, with the attention it places on right relationship, as the most effective kind of prevention for abuse. It communicates clearly that, in your congregation, sexualized abuse of any kind is never okay. It can also deepen your understanding of how you want to be in religious community, what your honest needs are, and what the limits are for behavior your community can contain.

Be prepared for people in your congregation to have a range of experiences and responses to this process. It is not only likely, but given the incidence in the general population, almost inevitable that your congregation has more than one person who is the survivor of sexual abuse. You may have a person or persons who is, or has been, an abuser in your community. Many people may be in denial about the importance of this issue. People will bring different agendas and a full range of emotional intensity. This issue touches deep places of pain, vulnerability, and therefore possibility for personal and spiritual growth. It can and should be an empowering experience for the congregation to be pro-active in reflecting on and addressing safety and right relations.

Leadership for a Creating Safe Congregations process can come from any committee or group of people in the congregation. Issues of safety may be most apparent, and deeply felt, by leaders in the religious education program, where issues of safety for children have high awareness. Or leadership may come from the Committee on Ministry, which should be aware of issues within the congregation or the experiences of clergy sexual misconduct in many denominations (including ours). A women's or men's spirituality group may take the lead. But for the covenant or promises to be most broadly owned, it is ideal if the governing body (parish committee, board of trustees, etc.) of the congregation owns the process. The following is a sample process, assuming that the congregational governing body initiates a congregational process.

The congregation's governing body decides to enter into a covenanting process. Before this action, members of the governing body have explored and considered the issues involved through the use of this workbook's material and/or with the help of the district's Safe Congregations Team. Throughout the decision-making process, information should be shared with the congregation.

The governing body has developed a process or plan to support those in the congregation—both abusers and survivors—recognizing that initiating this process signals a willingness on the part of the congregation and its leadership to deal openly with these realities.

The decision is shared with the congregation. The work of congregation-wide covenanting begins with a worship service that invites and encourages people to make commitments to one another about the creation and sustenance of right relations and safe spaces.

Sections of this workbook are used as resources for congregation-wide small group processes. These groups could be gathered around areas of common concern and responsibility, such as religious education, the Committee on Ministry, the Caring Committee or its equivalent, the Social Justice/Responsibility Committee.

Each small group reports regularly to the governing body as it moves through the process, indicating what is being done, how it is proceeding, what learning and changes are happening. Information on the process and work of covenanting is shared regularly and in many ways with the congregation. Each small group is asked to describe its vision for how the congregation will create and sustain right relations and safe spaces, outlining items they believe should be a part of the congregational covenant and the steps required to honor the covenant. The groups should pay special attention to their roles in this work. As the small groups make their pilgrimages in the covenanting process, these questions can prompt them to deeper engagement:

- What qualities do we want in our life together?

- What aspects of our life together foster right relations? What aspects threaten right relations?

- What aspects of our life together foster safety? What aspects threaten safety?

- What in our life together gives us the strength and courage to keep the promises we make to one another?

- What is my/our role in promise keeping?

- How will we keep this covenant alive over time? as new people join the community? as leadership changes? as the congregation changes?

A team of congregational members, appointed by the governing body, reviews input from the small group processes and prepares a covenant to propose to the congregation. The team may suggest language to add to the congregational mission or vision if these already exist.

The team's covenant statement should include specific steps that the congregation needs to take to move toward the creation and sustenance of right relations and safe spaces. The covenant is presented at a congregational meeting, along with a report from the team on its work and that of the small groups. After presentation and discussion, a vote is taken.

A worship service led by the minister(s) and members of the covenant team celebrates the covenant.

The governing body may appoint an ongoing covenant working group charged with encouraging, supporting, and helping to create opportunities for the congregation to keep the promises embodied in the covenant. The working group can assist committees and groups in incorporating the covenant into their work and planning.

Covenants are living documents that embody promises made by members of the community to one another. The Safe Congregations covenant therefore needs to be revisited and reviewed. There should be a clear understanding of how and when this review will take place. Because of the importance of this work, some congregations have found that scheduling an annual worship service on this theme provides an appropriate space to affirm the importance of this work to the community and suggest areas where the congregation has further work to do. This process may be especially important for congregations that not only have covenanted to prevent abuse, but are also in the process of healing after an instance of abuse.

The above suggestions can, of course, be modified to fit the needs of a congregation. Energy for this work can come from any source. There is no need for a slavish adherence to a particular sequence or structure. To engage in an intentional process around right relations and safe spaces as a congregation can be an empowering element in congregational life, providing (as in the case of the congregation in Gretchen Thomas's story—see Session 4) a sense and a reality that the congregation is moving toward greater honesty and accountability and being responsible about its life as a religious community.

It is with that hope and in that faith that this program is offered. We cannot guarantee safety, nor promise to heal all the wounds that persons bring with them when they cross the threshold of our communities. We can promise to hold on to the vision of right relationship and understand that we are called to create communities that are as safe as we can make them, so that our communities can be ones where personal transformation and greater spiritual depth are not only possible, but expected.

William Sinkford

Unitarian Universalist Resources on Sexual Abuse

Unitarian Universalist Association of Congregations At-Large

UUA Board of Trustees

The Board of Trustees is an elected governing body of the Unitarian Universalist Association and is responsible for the policies of the Association. It appoints committees and task forces to carry on their work and services.

In 1992, the UUA Board of Trustees appointed a Task Force on Congregational Response to Clergy Sexual Misconduct. This task force of five, known as Task Force II, was charged with creating materials to deal with congregational responses to the issue of clergy sexual misconduct and to make recommendations concerning laity education. This UUA Task Force is distinct and different in its charge from The Clearing House Task Force on Clergy Sexual Misconduct, known as Task Force I. For more information about the initial call to action in 1991 by the Board of the Unitarian Universalist Women's Federation and the UUA Women and Religion Committee, see the listing for the Unitarian Universalist Women's Federation under Associate Member Organizations in this section. Excerpts from Task Force II's final report follow.

Task Force on Congregational Response to Clergy Sexual Misconduct

Final Report to the Board of Trustees
October, 1994

Introduction

The journey of this task force began in the spring of 1992. With this report in the fall of 1994, we bring our work to a close. The responsibility of the Unitarian Universalist Association, however, in addressing this issue continues. Within the religious community, courageous voices broke the silence, naming this issue long before the task force was formed. They will continue to call for justice making within our religious movement. We must heed the call. The health of our religious community demands a compassionate and effective response.

Of the many dimensions of this work—personal, social, political, organizational, and spiritual—we urge particular attention to the spiritual. It is by building on our life-affirming theology that we will find our way to new understanding. Our ethical standards and definitions of justice exist in an evolving cultural context. We must stay open to new meanings, learning to forgive ourselves and others when past behaviors don't live up to new standards. We must be willing to speak the truth when it is difficult; and we must listen and learn from each other. Our understanding of the dynamics of power in human relationships is changing. Roles and responsibilities in human relationships have been redefined dramatically in the last decades. These are challenging times; and the faith that has supported us during past personal and community challenges will support us as we move through this one—if we draw on the principles we have in common. As Unitarian Universalists we are called to deepen our understanding and expand our vision. Our living tradition guides our search for justice. . . .

In Summary

In responding to the charge of the UUA Board, members of the task force have turned to personal, cultural, and theological sources for wisdom and guidance. Thus we bring our recommendations forward. Although we make several, each is closely related to the other and they are all part of one major recommendation.

The Unitarian Universalist Association and its affiliate organizations should undertake concerted and comprehensive strategies that:

1. increase awareness and understanding regarding the adverse impact that clergy sexual misconduct has on the affected individuals and congregations;
2. promote a well-publicized, coordinated institutional response to alleged misconduct to ensure justice making and support healing on the part of all involved; and
3. provide resources to congregations and individuals to foster the development of healthy ministries and safe, sacred congregations.

Specifically, responsibility for developing and distributing resources and for coordinating the delivery of services to member congregations should reside with the Department of Congregational, District, and Extension Services.

Further, the Association should work with the Ministerial Fellowship Committee, the UU Ministers Association, the UU Women's Federation, and other affiliate groups to ensure ongoing dialogue, input, and coordination of efforts. There is great risk that we become polarized as ministers and laypeople on this issue. Leadership from throughout the denomination must speak out to name the wrong and promote healing. The Association and its affiliate organizations must demonstrate an understanding that the well-being of congregations and the well-being of our ministers are intertwined.

Submitted by:

Janis Sabin Elliot, Chair	Donna DiSciullo
Portland, OR	Princeton, NJ
Elinor Artman	Michelle Hunt
Cincinnati, OH	Ewing, NJ
Thomas Mikelson	Kay Montgomery, Staff
Cambridge, MA	Boston, MA

Background

In 1984 and 1985, UUMA Chapters in the southeast and the Pacific northwest became concerned about the effects of ministerial sexual misconduct on congregations and ministry. They asked the UUMA Executive Committee to address sexual ethics in the ministerial Code of Professional Practice. After study and discussion, the Code was amended in 1987 and 1988 to include sexual ethics. The Ministerial Fellowship Committee used this Code as a basis for addressing the issue of clergy sexual misconduct.

In the spring of 1991, the issue of clergy sexual abuse took on an increased urgency in the Unitarian Universalist Association. Reports were mounting in the media and several incidents of misconduct within the denomination further focused the attention on this problem. Reactions were varied and intense: Many denied that a liberal religious community, one that affirmed an open, positive view of human sexuality, could be so afflicted by abuses of power. Others were enraged at an apparent institutional unwillingness to confront the issue or to hold offenders accountable, and resolved to effect change. Still others remained blissfully unaware of the problem within the denomination, agreeing that clergy sexual misconduct was wrong, but of the opinion that it wasn't that much of a problem in the UUA. The Task Force on Clergy Sexual Misconduct, now often referred to as Task Force One, formed as a response to discussions held at General Assembly in Hollywood, Florida, in 1991. Members in Task Force One came from the Unitarian Universalist Women's Federation (UUWF), the UU Women and Religion Committee, Ministerial Sisterhood UU (MSUU), Unitarian Universalist Ministers Association (UUMA), Liberal Religious Educators' Association (LREDA), the Department of Ministry, the UUA administration, and other interested groups and individuals. Task Force One served as a clearing house for information on clergy sexual misconduct. Among other things, it called on the UUA Board to pay attention to the needs of congregations. Into this context came the Task Force on Congregational Response to Clergy Sexual Misconduct.

This task force was created by the UUA Board of Trustees in January 1992. The increase in the reported incidence of clergy sexual misconduct (of 22 complaints between 1984 and 1994 involving sexual ethics issues, 13 took place between 1990 and 1993) brought a growing awareness of the effect of such misconduct on congregations and on ministry. This awareness resulted in demands that the Unitarian Universalist Association attend to the needs of its member congregations. Many people felt that more attention was being given to the ministers' needs and concerns than to those of congregations. It was time for balance. The Ministerial Fellowship Committee and the Department of Ministry had begun responding to this issue by revising the policies and procedures by which allegations against ministers were handled, but congregations were still left largely uninformed and unsupported. The Board's charge to the task force was to "create programs to deal with congregational response to ministerial sexual misconduct and to make recommendations concerning an education program for lay leaders designed to supplement and support the training being done with ministers on this issue. . . ."

Early Results—
Three Projects

Task force members immediately solicited input and information from across the denomination. It conducted a hearing at the General Assembly in Calgary in 1992. Lay leaders from affected congregations, staff from several Unitarian Universalist Association departments, District Field Services staff who had worked with congregations suffering from the trauma of clergy misconduct, and concerned Unitarian Universalists from all over the continent shared their opinions, ideas, and suggestions. It became immediately clear that while the true solutions would take time to implement throughout the denomination, it was important to start immediately to provide resources to congregations. The focus of the task force work would be on prevention, intervention, and healing in congregations. While task force members expected to identify areas other than congregational life that needed attention, priority would be given to congregations.

In that light, work began immediately on three projects:

1. Building a theological basis for the work. One of the first projects was the publication of a document, "Finding Our Way," which identified resources, including those from 38 other denominations, that might shape and inform our efforts. Published by the Unitarian Universalist Women's Federation, the authors called for theologies of sexuality that speak to the complex dynamics of sex and power, take seriously the horrific trauma experienced by survivors of sexual abuse, and remain sex-positive, open, and celebratory of the power of pleasure and eros in our individual and communal lives.

Thomas Mikelson and Donna DiSciullo worked with the Sexual Ethics Seminar to develop a discussion paper, "Reflections Toward a Unitarian Universalist Understanding of Clergy Sexual Abuse." The paper intends to stimulate discussion and understanding on the part of laity and clergy of the theological basis for the denomination. The task force urges dissemination of the paper and suggests that the Department of Religious Education and the Department of Ministry encourage its use throughout the denomination. (See copy of essay at the end of this report.)

2. Creating district resource and response teams. Late in 1991, the UUMA sponsored training for clergy by Marie Fortune of the Center for the Prevention of Sexual and Domestic Violence. Twenty clergy teams were trained; they, in turn, trained UUMA chapters throughout the Association. The task force designed a training program for district field services staff and lay leadership to build the capacity of our districts to provide consultation and assistance to congregations. The Resource and Response Team trainings created a congregational focus on the UUMA trainings and built clergy-laity partnerships. The three-day sessions are based on materials from the Center for the Prevention of Sexual and Domestic Violence on clergy misconduct and sexual abuse in the ministerial relationship with an emphasis on applying the materials to meet the needs of congregations. Three trainings were held during 1994. The response of participants was very positive. The Department of Congregational, District, and Extension Services is encouraged to provide the training on an ongoing basis.

3. Developing resources for congregations. A packet for congregations containing information about UUA policies and practices, resource people within and outside of the denomination, and recommended reading and worship resources to help congregations build a spiritual, justice-oriented base to this work was prepared by the task force. The packet "Re-Weaving the Threads, A Movement Toward Wholeness" is available from the Department of Congregational, District, and Extension Services.

Our Learnings

. . . . The Task Force discovered several basic principles and assumptions that underlie its work and guided its recommendations to the UUA Board of Trustees.

1. Prevention, intervention, and healing are integrally related. To effectively respond to clergy sexual misconduct in the denomination and to assist congregations, we must attend to three tasks concurrently: prevention strategies; intervention and response when misconduct occurs or is alleged; and support for healing in congregations and with individuals affected so that they can move on. Each is grounded in the elements of justice making, for there can be no healing without justice. The elements of justice making are described by Marie Fortune in the book *Is Nothing Sacred: When Sex Invades the Pastoral Relationship*: truth-telling—give voice to the reality of the abuse; acknowledge the violation—hear the truth, name the abuse, and condemn it as wrong; compassion—listen to and suffer with the victim; protect the vulnerable—take steps to prevent further abuse (including retaliation for speaking out); accountability—confront the abuse and impose negative consequences; restitution—make symbolic restoration of what was lost, give a tangible means to acknowledge the harm done; vindication—set the victim free from the suffering caused by the abuse.

2. There is no quick fix. This work is ongoing. It takes time to build the supports and structures needed to make things right. The task force's efforts are only the beginning of denominational work in this area. As an institution, we must be willing to sustain our efforts.

3. Build on strengths. A great deal is already going on in the denomination and society as a whole to address sexual abuse in general and clergy sexual misconduct in particular. It is important to acknowledge those efforts and build upon them. Much of that work is included in the resource packet prepared by the task force.

4. Healthy, safe congregations are the common goal; the underlying goal of our work is to support healthy ministries and safe congregations. We come to religious community for a variety of reasons, but are always in need of a safe, supportive environment within which we can explore our deeper selves. Congregations must, even more than the greater society, be safe from abuse and exploitation.

5. Look at the whole picture. An effective response must take into account all aspects of congregational life. Thus a holistic perspective is essential. We cannot point the finger of blame and take care of the problem. Individuals must be accountable for their actions, but true prevention and healing is about understanding and changing the nature of relationships within our institutions. In that light, we must all look at our roles and responsibilities.

6. Keep the work grounded. The work done by the Center for the Prevention of Sexual and Domestic Violence, particularly as it relates to clergy sexual abuse, is valid and useful to Unitarian Universalists. The concepts of healthy boundaries, professional standards and ethics, and justice making as central to healing and recovery should guide our efforts. The writings of Marie Fortune, in particular *Is Nothing Sacred?,* are recommended reading for all lay and ministerial leadership. The training available through the Center for the Prevention of Sexual and Domestic Violence provide a core to efforts in prevention and intervention.

7. Congregations are the focus, but the principles are useful in other areas. The charge of this task force is directed toward congregations and incidents of clergy sexual misconduct. We recognize that sexual abuse by members of the church community other than clergy and staff (church members, volunteers, family members) is also of concern in our religious communities. Indeed many of us have experienced sexual abuse in our lives; that history affects our response to clergy misconduct. Our findings and recommendations relate to clergy misconduct for it sets the tone and the capacity of the church to respond to other situations. What we learn here helps us extend our work into other aspects of sexual abuse and violence in our societies and the culture as a whole.

8. The congregations' voice must be heard. In all aspects of this work, the Association must ensure the presence of a congregational voice. Laypeople must be included on all committees, task forces, and meetings. Congregational representatives will keep the work grounded by voicing their sense of realities and consequences.

9. Every situation is different, yet all have some things in common. In the process of our work as a task force, we confirmed the truth of what we believed to be true. While individual circumstances surrounding the situations of clergy sexual misconduct may vary, there are many common characteristics.

People are affected in many ways when clergy sexual misconduct occurs, whether it becomes public knowledge, and our denomination must attend to the needs of all affected parties. The best representation of this holistic approach can be found in "Primary Elements in a Systems Approach to Prevention and Response to Clergy Sexual Misbehavior" published by the Episcopal church. . . . It identifies the affected parties and what resources are needed to respond to them. It is incumbent on our societies, district field offices, UUMA chapters, and the departments of the UUA to ensure that the needs of all are addressed.

Keeping secrets and avoiding the issue will not work. The problem is compounded when boards and offending ministers work out mutual agreements that try to find a solution without facing the misconduct. It usually comes back to haunt us. The issue must be named and confronted.

Although difficult, there are respectful, honest, and compassionate ways through the situation. We must, however, do the hard work of living our principles and purposes and learn how to confront hard truths with each other. Preventive procedures and policies can help, as can getting help from the outside. Churches and ministers cannot and should not try to handle this alone.

There are success stories to be told. We are learning how to respond and we need to tell each other what we've done that helps. We also have many resource people to whom we can turn for guidance. The task of the UUA, both in Boston and in the field, is to network and help congregations access those resources.

We are naive at best if we think our liberal religious tradition exempts us from this problem. There is no reason to believe we are any worse or any better in this regard. It is incumbent on us to understand the nature of the relationship between minister and congregation and to confront directly the effect on individuals, members, congregations, and the entire religious movement when abuse occurs.

Recommendation　The UUA should institutionalize an ongoing response to clergy sexual misconduct. A vision of healthy ministries and safe and sacred congregations inspires this recommendation. Working to achieve that vision is to the benefit of the Association, its member societies, and individual Unitarian Universalists.

Within this recommendation we identify a number of ways in which the UUA can assume responsibility in all areas of the institution. Effective action is not the responsibility of only one or two departments. The work does not belong only to the Association: Its member societies and affiliate organizations must also share in the work. We fully expect that this work will be taken up in a variety of ways by many different voices within our denomination. Doing so is vital to achieving our goal of healthy, safe communities within which we can minister to each other and to the world. It is the responsibility of the UUA to provide the moral, spiritual, and institutional leadership required.

Responsibility for developing and distributing resources and for coordinating delivery of services to member congregations should reside with the Department of Congregational, District, and Extension Services. Among these responsibilities are to:

- Attend to the needs of victims and congregations. To provide clear, timely information to congregations involved in a report of clergy sexual misconduct, the department should designate a staff member to coordinate assistance to a congregation and keep in touch with the victim(s). The designated staff person (which could be a different person for different situations) will coordinate the flow of information within the UUA and ensure that congregational leadership gets clear, timely answers about the process and that congregations have access to resource materials about clergy sexual misconduct.

- Respond quickly with information and assistance. The department must make crisis consultation and intervention services available to affected congregations. These services should be closely coordinated with the district executive, but not be delivered by the district staff. Field staff may be more helpful in promoting healing and prevention if they are not directly involved with crisis services.

- Identify resource people. There are many trained and qualified volunteers around the continent who may help the department in assisting a congregation during the process. There is a pool of qualified, capable, and interested persons (clergy and laity) who can be recruited to assist the department and member congregations. These volunteers, for a stipend and expenses, can provide a calm presence and assist church boards, district field staff, and the UUA in determining what will be most helpful. In some cases, this support could be provided by telephone consultation.

- Provide ongoing training to district and congregational leadership. The training model developed by the Task Force for Resource and Response Teams should be offered. Districts should be encouraged to offer training for search committees, committees on ministry, leadership schools, and other appropriate groups. Different components of the training (i.e., preventive strategies, handling crises) could be offered in different settings.

- Maintain and distribute resource packets prepared by the task force. These packets should be made available at nominal expense through the UUA Bookstore. All congregations should be informed of their availability.

- Coordinate the UUA's efforts: The department must ensure ongoing coordination and cooperation among the departments of the UUA to ensure that congregations are well served. At a minimum, the staff clearing house on sexual abuse and misconduct issues should be continued. Representatives should come from the following departments: ministry; religious education; district, congregational, and extension services; youth; and faith in action.

Comments and Suggestions

The charge to the task force was to focus on congregations. We believe that the Department of Congregational, District, and Extension Services is best equipped to carry out those responsibilities. Other departments and denominational committees also have special responsibilities to member congregations. The following recommendations pertain to them.

1. Ministerial Fellowship Committee (MFC): In addition to the changes in policies and procedures relating to clergy sexual misconduct already adopted by the MFC, the task force recommends the following:

   - The MFC should require preparation in professional ethics as a requirement of preliminary fellowship. While our seminaries now include seminars on professional ethics as part of ministerial education, many clergy enter our ministry through other paths. The common point for all is the MFC.
   - A discussion of professional ethics should be included as a criteria for final fellowship. By doing so, committees on ministry and church boards will also become more informed about the topic and aware of the denomination's professional standards.
   - The MFC should include a book on sexual ethics on the required reading list. The task force recommends *Is Nothing Sacred: When Sex Invades the Pastoral Relationship* by Marie Fortune.
   - Ministers who apply for re-credentialing after being dropped from Fellowship because of sexual misconduct should make restitution to the victim(s) as a requirement of the re-credentialing.

- A "no probable cause" finding after an allegation of ministerial misconduct should be made public.

2. The Department of Ministry should:

   - Develop training for search committees about professional sexual ethics.
   - Have ministerial settlement representatives walk through the UUMA guidelines with the search committee.
   - Review the policy on the accessibility of information in a minister's file relating to sexual misconduct. Consider including information regarding a charge of clergy sexual misconduct and the resolution of that charge in the information provided to search committees.
   - Provide specialized training to interim ministers on the effects of abuse on the congregation and strategies to help congregations recover from the abuse.

3. The Unitarian Universalist Ministers Association: The willingness of the UUMA to volunteer its time to train the District Resource and Response Teams evidences its interest and commitment. Leadership must come from all sectors to speak to the importance of addressing the issue and to increasing understanding that the well-being of ministers and the well-being of congregations are intertwined. The UUMA is encouraged to continue work with lay leadership in this area. Educated, informed, and involved laypeople are vital partners with ministers in building healthy ministries and safe congregations.

4. Unitarian Universalist Women's Federation and affiliated organizations: These organizations gave voice to those within our religious movement who said "no more." The task force recognizes the important role they have played in furthering this work, in creating the climate within which we could carry out our task, and in building the safety where dialogue and learning could take place. We recommend the continuation of Task Force One and encourage other voices to join in.

The work of the task force has ended but the work of the denomination is only beginning. The affect that clergy sexual abuse has on us all is significant. It undermines the very foundation of congregational life. We are challenged to learn and grow from our explorations of the issues involved. It is hard work, for it involves a deep, intensely personal understanding of the way power works in our own lives and how we are affected by the use and abuse of power by those we trust. When we understand this, we can move significantly forward in our quest for justice and balance in the world. The task force concluded early in our exploration that the work we are called to do in redressing the wrongs of clergy sexual abuse and in healing our congregations is applicable in all other areas of our religious journey together. It will serve us well as we seek racial and economic justice, respect for our environment and those who share it with us, and the deeper understanding of our spiritual selves. The Chinese character for crises consists of two symbols: danger and opportunity. The danger is that this issue will undermine the basis of trust and justice upon which we build our religious movement. The opportunity is that we will learn to relate to each other in new ways and transform the nature of our experience.

> In that spirit,
> May we never end our efforts
> > to bring greater understanding to our world
> > to offer justice to those injured by power-over
> > to speak truth to power
> > > with awareness of our human limitations
> > > and an abiding belief
> > > > in the possibility of redemption
> Through healing love. So be it! Blessed be!

Discussion Essay   *Reflections Toward a Unitarian Universalist Theological Understanding of Clergy Sexual Abuse*
Thomas Mikelson

1. For Unitarian Universalists, a congregation is a primary locus of value, commitment, and hope, a place where we hope to find the spirit of God.

Unitarian Universalists grant to congregations extensive authority and accord them our most solemn respect. We strengthen our religious tradition by strengthening congregations or forming new ones. Congregations have been the creators and bearers of traditions. There is no creed or dogma that takes precedence over the congregation, no hierarchy whose authority transcends the authority of the congregation, not even a ministry whose collective wisdom is considered weightier than the wisdom of persons in congregations.

A congregation is a primary religious and theological point of reference, a gathering place to experience and refine and preserve cherished values. We gather in congregations because we have faith that there attention will be directed toward life's real and deeper experiences—birth and death, relationship, community, personal and communal struggles, the meaning of work. In a congregation, we expect the ultimate mystery of life to be acknowledged and held in honor. We expect the shared life of a congregation to focus on a deeper appreciation of that mystery, to celebrate it, and to help us bring our personal lives into accord with the best understanding of it.

The term God and other analogous terms are metaphors for that power that reaches toward the highest in life. We believe that the search for God (or whatever term is preferred to indicate the mystery that sustains our existence) is best enhanced by life in a community of faith, a congregation. We want life in the congregation to be ordered in ways that enable our search for the sacred and enhance our respect for it.

2. Congregations are gathered in covenant.

A Unitarian Universalist congregation is gathered by the consent of its members, who agree to walk together in a unity of spirit. In our liberal ecclesiology (how we organize and relate to one another in congregations), the principles of "consent," "walking together," and "unit of spirit" provide the basis for a congregation as community. The covenant of any congregation may express more than this, more detail in content, but it may not suggest less than this.

3. Ministry is brought into being by congregations, which confers upon them the powers which attend ministry.

Ministers are called to provide leadership in religious community; a ministry has its beginning in that call. The power of ministry, therefore, is rooted first in the power of a congregation. A congregation possesses power to call a minister but ministers possess no similar authority organizationally that take precedence over the will of a congregation. Ministry is created by the call of a congregation, not vice versa; the congregation remains the primary circle of reference for ministry. Implicitly in the call of a minister, of course, is the notion of a minister's inner authority, the minister's "call" to ministry. When a minister is called by a congregation, it is agreed that the minister will speak freely and without censure out of inner conviction and authority. We symbolize that inner authority in the metaphor "free pulpit." In the exercise of a free pulpit, a minister has considerable power to move and influence a congregation. A congregation assumes priority over that authority only in the sense that it first called the minister and can, at any time, terminate that minister's call. This order of authority is basic to religious life in our left-wing protestant tradition.

4. Life in a spiritual community heightens personal vulnerability.

Congregations gather for the purposes of spiritual life and work, both personal and communal. "Walking together in a unity of spirit" is a metaphor for that spiritual work. Spiritual work means deepening self understanding, growing clarity about purpose and commitment, and increasing awareness of how our lives are interconnected morally with the web of creation. Spiritual work, the transformation of self and world, leads both inward and outward; inward to confrontations with ourselves, outward to issues of justice. Implicitly in the shared life of creation, spiritual work requires self awareness and dialogue, speaking and listening, and continuing interaction. Within the community of faith, as spiritual work proceeds, individuals become better known to one another, more transparent, more open to critical response; members become more vulnerable and defenses fall away. A spiritual community, therefore, is a place where persons are more opened to risk.

5. *The work of religious community is to create and preserve the safety and trust in which spiritual growth can occur.*

In our congregations, we expect to be safe, not to have to be constantly on guard, as we have to be often in daily life, against the possibilities of exploitation and abuse. Spiritual growth leads persons back and forth between the faith community and the work outside, between risk and security, between being tested and being nurtured. The rhythm of spiritual life is supported best by the sort of safety rarely found outside of religious community. Safety from abuse is one of the identifying signs of a healthy spiritual community. The fact that we gather in communities of faith suggests, beyond our hunger for spiritual growth, a need for safety that allows us to let down defenses that usually stand in the way of self-examination. We can allow ourselves to be vulnerable only when we are reasonably confident that others in our communities will not take advantage of our vulnerability.

For some, trust refers to a component of specific relationships; it means that they find this or that person trustworthy. For others, trust is a reality that can transcend individuals; it refers to the spiritual quality of an entire community. They sense that a community is trustworthy or not. For still others, trust is a way of pointing to something sacred, something in the nature of God, something which, while they may participate in it and foster it through their ways of relating, is beyond them and makes it possible for them to trust in the first place. For them, trust may be a symbol for God; "God is trust." Unitarian Universalists will disagree about the ways of expressing what trust means to us, but we can agree about the necessity of trust as a context and precondition of spiritual community.

6. *Violation of trust fractures spiritual community.*

Unitarian Universalists have inherited the Judeo-Christian tradition that holds that repentance and forgiveness can restore relationships and communities that have been traumatized by mistrust and betrayal. That should not blind us to the fact that breaches of trust cut deeply into the cushion of good will that buffer life in any healthy community and such breaches are profoundly difficult to heal. In religious community, breach of trust damages the very condition required for spiritual work, just as breach of trust between persons inhibits the growth and exploration. We cannot make ourselves vulnerable where we lack trust in the safety of our context. In the order of Unitarian Universalist values, few violations are more egregious than undermining the foundations of religious community. Damage to the trust that makes community possible is not simply an offense against an individual with private consequences; it is an offense against community, an offense which undermines and fractures community. Trust can be damaged as easily through silence and deception as through intentional acts. Silence or deception about abusive behavior or breaches of professional ethics is a violation of trust and damages the safety of a community over and above the original violation.

7. Ministry is a fiduciary relationship.

What is trust about? Trust is the precondition of spiritual community. Trust is the basis of ministry. Ministry is a fiduciary relationship. We are bound by our calling as ministers to act for the benefit of others in matters connected with our ministry. A fiduciary relation is founded in trust or confidence reposed by one party in the integrity and fidelity of another. A fiduciary relation arises whenever confidence is understood by both parties to have been reposed in one of the parties with the result that the other party is vulnerable or, in some ways, dependent. The words spoken by members of a congregation when they install or ordain a new minister provide a clear example of one party conferring upon another, by virtue of office, the confidence of a fiduciary relationship. If congregations are spiritual communities and ministers are called to lead spiritual communities and serve in the role of spiritual directors, then ministers assume a fiduciary responsibility to guard the safety of the congregation for all members. Ministers need to be sensitive to how intimate friendships with congregants, especially if they become sexualized, can destroy the minister's fiduciary responsibilities both to those specific friends and to the larger congregation.

8. There are many roles in ministry.

There are many roles in ministry: pastor, preacher, teacher, keeper of traditions, counselor, prophetic voice, community representative, mediator, facilitator, artist, liturgist. The roles of ministry vary from congregation to congregation and tradition to tradition, but there are always roles in ministry. Within congregations, ministers cannot stand outside those roles or the suggestive images which surround those roles. The roles have a history apart from any minister; they belong, in large part, to the shared tradition or the congregation and they have power that transfers to any minister who is called to assume them.

9. There is power in ministerial roles and relationships.

A minister participates in a power network within a congregation. Congregations confer powers upon their ministers through roles that the minister is expected to assume—worship leader, teacher, counselor, officiant at life's most meaningful ceremonies of passage, representative in the larger community. A minister is expected to understand that she or he is a trustee of those powers, not their author or owner.

The powers of ministry have potential for good if they are used responsibly, and potential for damage if they are abused. The powers of ministry are not well understood; ministers themselves frequently believe that ministry is lacking in power. Those who do not recognize and understand the powers of ministry are more likely to exercise those powers irresponsibly. It is important, therefore, in the formation of ministers, to instill a full appreciation of the powers of ministry.

10. Unitarian Universalists approach our spiritual lives as people who fully affirm sexual pleasure and responsible sexual relationships.

Unitarian Universalists have sought, often against reactionary currents in the larger society, to uphold erotic sexuality as fully and positively human. We teach our children that sexual pleasure is beautiful and powerful and that they can combine full sexual enjoyment with responsible sexual behavior. We create communities of faith that include people who are openly gay, lesbian, bisexual, and straight. We approach our spiritual lives as people who fully affirm sexual pleasure and responsible sexual relationships. We believe that healthy sexuality contributes to a fuller life. We do not set religious leaders apart as nonsexual or less-sexual persons. Ministers are fully erotic persons, like everyone else, and we expect them, like everyone else, to be responsible in their sexual relationships. Ministers, because they lead communities of faith, bear the additional responsibility to guard the safety of congregations from abuse and the integrity of ministry from degrading ridicule.

11. Because spirituality and sexuality are so interrelated, ministers must be responsible for setting limits on the religio-erotic power of ministry.

Ministers regularly assume roles which congregants view as powerful and attractive. Ministers deal with life's most intimate experiences—birth, death, dedication of life, marriage, coming of age, personal stress, crises of family and work, and many more. They are welcomed into people's homes and private spaces, and are entrusted with the most personal information on others' lives. These unique characteristics of ministry enhance the attractiveness of ministers to congregants and contribute to the positive, healing potential of ministry. But the same characteristics also increase the power of ministers over congregants, and thus the risks of abuse.

Spiritual work often requires the baring of souls and can be intimate, leaving congregants vulnerable. Congregants may need to share intimate information about their lives with a minister; but the area of shared, two-way intimacy is a special danger in minister-congregant relationships. Congregants need assurance that their minister's attention is focused on meeting the congregant's need, not the personal needs of the minister. Ministers can be warm and receptive without sharing their own personal intimacies.

Religio-erotic power is a potentially positive source of influence in ministry. There is nothing morally wrong with appropriate intimacy in ministerial relationships, and there is nothing morally wrong with religio-erotic power in ministry; but there is everything wrong with abuse of that intimacy and power. When appropriate intimacy in a ministerial relationship is exceeded for the sake of sexual activity or sexualized behavior between minister and congregant, the result is clergy sexual abuse. The ethic of ministry demands that responsibility for setting appropriate boundaries of intimacy belongs to the minister.

12. Sexual relationships or sexualized behavior between a minister and a congregant are abuses of clergy power and authority.

The power associated with roles of ministry makes any relationship between a minister and a congregant unequal. Congregants, though they may have their own kinds of power to wield in relationships, still do not possess the powers of a minister. A minister always possesses power in such relationships, which a congregant does not have. Because of that power imbalance, sexual relationships or sexualized behavior between a minister and a congregant constitute an abuse of ministerial authority.

When a minister develops a sexual relationship with a member of her or his congregation, their sexual relationship preempts the usual minister/congregant relationship; the congregant loses a minister. The congregant in such a situation is often alienated from the congregation, losing both minister and congregation. Victims of clergy sexual abuse also report that spiritual life is damaged; the abuse closes a door between the victim and God, between the victim and her or his sources of spiritual nurture.

Clergy sexual abuse disturbs the larger network of relationships in a congregation. Some may fear that they too could become victims of the minister's inappropriate behavior; others may wish they too could have an intimate or sexual relation with the minister. In addition to the personal damage to the immediate victim, disruption of the congregation damages the essential climate of trust required for spiritual community, eroding not just the minister's effectiveness but the overall ministry of the congregation. All of this, collectively, is the consequence of clergy sexual abuse.

13. Any violation of ministry goes to the integrity of ministry itself.

Ministry enjoys a distinguished tradition conveyed over time by those who have respectfully taken up its roles and responsibly exercised its powers. There is an expectation, when candidates enter the ministry, that they will uphold the integrity of the office to which they have been called. The collegial circle of the ministry depends on trust, in much the same way as any community of faith is a circle dependent on trust. No violation of professional ethics is isolated; any violation of ministry goes to the integrity of ministry itself. Any abuse of a ministerial relationship can be felt far and wide as a violation of the integrity of ministry, extending throughout a city or region, or an entire denomination. Clergy sexual abuse is abuse of the role of the minister as well as abuse of those who are victims.

14. *The victims of clergy sexual abuse are any who are hurt by it.*

In any case of clergy sexual abuse, there is an immediate and compelling concern about the immediate victim(s). But they are not the only victims. It already has been said that the circle of ministry is damaged by that abuse; ministers are victims of other ministers' abuse. We are also beginning to understand, through experience, that congregations are victims of clergy sexual abuse. When a fiduciary relationship of ministry is broken, the congregation will almost certainly experience a trauma of loss and betrayal.

We know now that a single case of clergy sexual abuse can trigger subsequent interactions within a congregation and that congregants who are not in any way originally involved are likely to be hurt (victimized) in the process. That happens in nearly every known case. We are beginning to understand these dynamics and the extent of victimization that results from clergy sexual abuse.

Ministerial Fellowship Committee

The Ministerial Fellowship Committee is a UUA Board-appointed standing committee. Its 15 members include ministers, lay leaders, and professionals, as well as two Board members. The Committee credentials ministers, sets standards for ministers, and disciplines ministers and ministerial students. It is governed by UUA bylaws and Ministerial Fellowship Committee rules and policies. The following excerpts include pertinent rules and policies on criteria and termination of fellowship.

Excerpts from MFC Rules, Bylaws, and Policies

24. Special Review Procedures
The Executive Secretary may, whenever he/she believes it necessary, present to the Ministerial Fellowship Committee the situation of any minister whose overall record seems to indicate that his or her continued recommendation for positions in societies or other institution by the Department of Ministry is not justified. The Committee shall itself study each situation thoroughly or appoint a subcommittee, which may include some persons who are not members of the Committee, to make such a study and report to the Committee. The Committee shall determine what action shall be taken by the Department of Ministry.

25. Criteria for Termination of Fellowship
The status of Fellowship of a minister of the Unitarian Universalist Association may be terminated upon the occurrence of any of these circumstances:

A. When the Committee is unable to locate the address of a minister for two consecutive years, the Committee shall make a record in summary form of its efforts to locate such person. Reinstatement may be made by the Committee upon location of a current address within a reasonable period of time.

B. When a minister who has been in Associate Fellowship for a period of three years or more fails to provide evidence of continued denominational involvement within sixty days of the Committee's letter of inquiry.

C. When a minister's performance and/or behavior in a society or any other professional position is found by the Committee to be conduct unbecoming a minister, or for other specified cause.

D. When a minister accepts settlement in a position for which he or she has not been certified by the Ministerial Fellowship Committee.

26. Procedures for Termination of Fellowship

The Committee shall institute proceedings to determine whether a minister's Fellowship status shall be terminated upon the receipt of information from any identified source that indicates the probability that one or more of the criteria for termination exists.

A. Rights of the Minister. The final fellowship of a minister may be suspended or terminated by the Ministerial Fellowship Committee for unbecoming conduct or other specified cause after notice and opportunity for a hearing before the Committee at which the minister shall have the right to be represented by counsel, to introduce evidence, to have any relevant and material evidence in the possession of the Association produced, and to cross-examine and rebut adverse evidence.

B. Rights of the Committee. The Committee shall also have the right to be represented by counsel, to introduce evidence, to have any relevant and material evidence in the possession of the minister produced, and to cross examine and rebut adverse evidence.

C. Expenses. All expenses involved in the travel, appearance, and representation of the minister charged and of the witnesses called in the minister's defense shall be borne by that minister.

D. Notice of Charges and Hearing. Except with respect to Rule 25 (A) and (B), upon a finding of probable cause the Committee shall notify the minister in writing of the charges that have been brought, the date and place when a hearing shall be held, the minister's rights, and the procedures that will be followed. Such notification shall be sent by certified mail and shall be postmarked not less than one month before the scheduled date of the hearing.

E. Response. Within fourteen (14) days of notice, the minister must advise the Committee whether or not she or he intends to appear at the hearing, whether or not she or he intends to be represented by an attorney and his or her identity, and the minister's response to the charges.

F. Exchange of Documents. Before the hearing, the minister and the Committee shall arrange for the mutual exchange of documents and a list of anticipated witnesses.

G. Criminal Proceedings. In the event that criminal charges are pending against the minister, the Executive Committee may suspend all or part of its investigation until the conclusion of the criminal adjudication. A court transcript or record may be used in lieu of or in addition to an investigative committee report.

H. Hearing Procedures.
    1. Hearing Panel. The hearing may be conducted by the Committee itself, with or without the assistance of counsel, or the Committee may appoint a Board of Inquiry to consist of three members, who need not be members of the Committee—for example, a member, an attorney at law, and one other person. When appointed, one of the three shall be designated as chair by the Ministerial Fellowship Committee.
    2. Confidentiality. At the beginning of the hearing, rules of confidentiality will be established and emphasized, and they will be reiterated at the end. All individuals—including Committee members, the person being heard, and the support person and/or counsel—must respect all rules of confidentiality.
    3. Record. The Board of Inquiry may determine if it wants a stenographic record at its own cost. If either party wants a stenographic record, it should notify the other three days before the hearings so that it can decide whether to (a) have its own stenographic record made, or (b) negotiate with the other party to share such. Every party shall pay the cost of the transcript. If either or both parties obtain a stenographic record, a copy shall also be obtained and paid for by the Ministerial Fellowship Committee.
    4. Procedures. The proceedings shall be conducted in such manner as the Committee or its Board of Inquiry shall determine within the limitations set forth above. The Committee or its Board of Inquiry shall have the authority to make any rulings on the conduct of the proceedings, including any rulings deemed necessary or appropriate to ensure that the hearings are conducted in an expeditious manner with due regard for the age and circumstances of the witnesses.

5. Recommendations of Board of Inquiry. If the proceedings are conducted by a Board of Inquiry appointed by the Committee, any findings of the Board of Inquiry together with the stenographic records and such reports as the Board of Inquiry may file shall be submitted to the Committee with its recommendations for decision. The chair of the Board of Inquiry shall be responsible for submitting this material, which shall be sent to the Committee not later than one calendar month from the date of the last day of the hearing.

6. Access to Information. All material sent to the Committee by the Board of Inquiry shall be open to inspection by the minister charged and/or a second person of the charged minister's choice.

7. Determination. The Committee, either at the conclusion of its own hearing, or upon receipt of the finding, etc., from the Board of Inquiry, shall determine whether the minister's status shall be terminated and shall enter in the record of the case the reasons for its decision and an order disposing of the case. Should the minister's Fellowship in the UUA not be terminated, the Committee may impose conditions and/or restrictions as it deems appropriate. Such decision shall be made at the next scheduled meeting of the Ministerial Fellowship Committee. Written notice of the decision containing the reasons thereof shall be sent by the Committee's executive secretary to the minister charged within seven days of the date of the decision.

8. Additional Proceedings. The Committee, at any time before the renderings of its decision, or prior to a final decision by the Review Panel in the event of appeal by the minister charged, shall have the power to reopen the proceedings to consider newly discovered evidence. In that event, the minister shall be notified in writing that the proceedings to terminate Fellowship have been reopened.

27. Appeals

In all cases involving termination of Fellowship, except those arising under Rule 25(A) and (B), the minister charged shall have the right of appeal and the following procedures shall be followed:

Any minister holding Final Fellowship whose Fellowship has been terminated may appeal to the Ministerial Fellowship Board of Review within thirty (30) calendar days. A minister who appeals as aforesaid agrees by so doing to abide by the bylaws of the Association pertaining to the Ministerial Fellowship Board of Review, and agrees that the final disposition of his or her appeal by said Board shall be binding upon him or her and that neither he or she nor his or her legal representative shall have any further recourse whatsoever in any proceeding within the Unitarian Universalist Association.

When an appeal is timely filed, the minister's status shall be that of "suspension from Ministerial Fellowship" until his or her case is finally disposed of, and during such suspension the minister's name shall not appear on lists of those in Ministerial Fellowship, and the minister shall not be recommended by the Department of Ministry. However, financial rights existing at the time of suspension, including any right to receive pension or insurance payments dependent upon Ministerial Fellowship, shall not be affected during the period of suspension.

Such an appeal shall be filed with the secretary of the Ministerial Fellowship Board of Review within thirty (30) calendar days of the decision of the Ministerial Fellowship Committee and in such form as said Board by its rules shall prescribe. If such an appeal is not filed in accordance with rules of the Board of Review, the ministers whose Fellowship status has been terminated agrees that the decision of the Ministerial Fellowship Committee shall be final and binding upon him or her and that neither he or she nor his or her legal representative shall have any further recourse whatsoever in any proceeding within the Unitarian Universalist Association.

If action by the Committee is affirmed, modified, or reversed upon appeal, the Committee shall take such action and make such entries on its records as required by any decision or order entered in the appeal proceedings.

28. Readmission

The Committee shall have authority to readmit a minister to membership in Ministerial Fellowship. An application on such form as the Committee shall determine shall be filed, said application to include in any event a brief statement of the reasons for termination of Fellowship status, and the reasons for readmission that the applicant believes should be considered. The decision on an application for readmission shall not be subject to appeal. Ordinarily an applicant for readmission will be required to comply with Rules 13 and 14, but the Committee may modify or waive any of said requirements.

30. Conviction Disclosure

Ministers in Fellowship with the Unitarian Universalist Association shall inform the Ministerial Fellowship Committee of all criminal convictions that occur subsequent to December 31, 1989, except for minor traffic violations and those convictions which by law they need not disclose.

Applicants for Fellowship with the Unitarian Universalist Association shall inform the Ministerial Fellowship Committee of all criminal convictions except for minor traffic violations and those convictions which by law they need not disclose. Such disclosure is required for Ministerial Fellowship.

31. Cooperating with the Committee

It is expected that all candidates for Fellowship and all ministers in

Fellowship will cooperate with the Committee at all times. This includes responses to requests for information, provision of requested documentation, and attendance at meetings with the Committee. Noncompliance may be deemed conduct unbecoming a minister.

Rules adopted by the UUA Board of Trustees April 1980; and amendments adopted June 1980, October 1980, April 1981, January 1983, January 1984, January 1986, October 1989, January 1989, April 1989, October 1989, January 1991, April 1991, January 1992, October 1993.

Board of Review

An elected UUA committee with seven members, the Board of Review receives and reviews appeals by ministers in final ministerial fellowship whose fellowship has been terminated at the determination of the Ministerial Fellowship Committee. The Board of Review has exclusive jurisdiction to hear and decide such appeals.

Women and Religion Committee

This Board-appointed committee was created as a result of the Women and Religion Resolution passed in 1977. This resolution urged the UUA and all Unitarian Universalists to look at the religious roots of sexism and to examine the extent to which religious beliefs influence sex-role stereotypes in interpersonal behavior in families, friendships, and work. The Women and Religion Committee was charged with overseeing the implementation of this resolution.

In 1991 at the General Assembly in Hollywood, Florida, the Committee and the Unitarian Universalist Women's Federation jointly issued a Call to Action on Clergy Sexual Misconduct. For more information about that call, see the Unitarian Universalist Women's Federation listed under Associate Member Organizations.

General Assembly Resolutions on Sexual Abuse and Interpersonal Violence

General Resolutions passed by the delegate body of the UUA General Assembly that focus on sexual abuse and interpersonal violence include the following: Child Abuse and Neglect—1977, Battered Women—1979, Implementation of Women and Religion Resolution—1980, On Children, Poverty, and Violence—1984, Sexual Abuse—1985, Supporting Legal Equity for Gays and Lesbians/The Welcoming Congregation—1987, Racial and Cultural Diversity in Unitarian Universalism—1992, Toward Safe Congregations and Right Relationships—1995, Violence Against Women—1993. The text of some resolutions is excerpted below.

Sexual Abuse

Passed by the UUA General Assembly in 1985.
Whereas, sexual abuse and exploitation of children and youth are continental problems; and

Whereas, the Unitarian Universalist Association is committed to affirm and promote the inherent worth and dignity of every person; and

Whereas, the Unitarian Universalist Association holds that sexual abuse and exploitation of children and youth are contrary to the principles of Unitarian Universalism and mentally, physically, emotionally, and spiritually harmful as well as moral and unethical; and

Whereas, the effects of sexual abuse and exploitation are long term, and healing is slow;

Be it resolved: That the 1985 General Assembly urges member congregations to explore the issues, causes, and treatments of the sexual abuse and exploitation of children and to encourage intergenerational programs which provide children with a positive, caring, open, and constructive relationship with adults; and

Be it further resolved: That this assembly urges the Religious Education Section to make available materials for children and youth providing information on how to protect themselves from sexual abuse and exploitation plus resources to help them if they have been abused or exploited; and

Be it further resolved: That this assembly urges the board of trustees of the association to develop, using qualified, expert, and involved sources, a code of ethics for persons working with youth and children for use in all UUA sponsored programs and as a model for congregations and districts to adopt.

Violence Against Women

Passed by the UUA General Assembly in 1993.
Because Unitarian Universalists affirm the inherent worth and dignity of every person, and living with dignity includes freedom from physical and emotional violence and the fear of such violence in the home, workplace, church, and community; and

Whereas the number of reported cases of harassment and stalking of women is increasing;

Whereas the rates of violent crime including sexual assault, rape, battering, and murder are rising and battering is the largest cause of injury to women in the United States and Canada;

Whereas violence against women occurs in families of all classes and races and is frequently perpetuated across generations;

Whereas violence against women is frequently trivialized, unreported, hidden within the family, or blamed on the victim;

Whereas our patriarchal system creates and sustains such violence by viewing and treating women as if they are of little value; and

Whereas the Unitarian Universalist sexism audits, "Checking Our Balance," and "Cleansing Our Temple," reveal our own continuing need to recognize patriarchal thinking and practices within us as individuals, among us in our congregations, and around us in society;

Therefore be it resolved that the Unitarian Universalist Association shall act and urge its associate members, affiliate organizations, member congregations, and individual Unitarian Universalists to:

1. break the silence by naming and speaking of the violence women experience in their homes, schools, work places, churches, and communities;
2. examine the nature and consequences of harassment and the ways in which our social, commercial, and religious institutions sanction harassment of women;
3. develop and implement educational programs for children and adults to empower individuals and groups to work at eliminating violence against women;
4. develop and implement programs to examine the roles that religious myths and institutions play in fostering violence or in healing its effects;
5. promote legislation to stop violence against women;
6. promote legislation to require that physicians report suspected cases of abuse;
7. advocate for the introduction of school curricula that promote gender equality and respect, and teach non-violent means of conflict resolution;
8. support the development and implementation of training programs for law enforcers, health-care providers, business and legal professionals, educators, child care workers, and clergy, to increase awareness of the causes and symptoms of violence against women and effective methods of intervention;
9. promote the creation of safe houses, shelters, counseling centers, and support groups for victims and their dependents; and
10. promote personal accountability through intervention and treatment programs, including individual and small group counseling for abusers.

Be it further resolved that the Unitarian Universalist Association shall act and urge its associate members, affiliate organizations, member congregations, and individual Unitarian Universalists to support the continental network, Unitarian Universalists Acting to Stop Violence Against Women, in its work, which includes congregation-based programs of worship, ritual, religious education, caring communities, and social action;

Be it further resolved that the 1993 General Assembly requests the President of the Unitarian Universalist Association to report annually on progress in implementing this resolution; and

Be it finally resolved that Unitarian Universalist congregations and individual Unitarian Universalists be urged to recognize the pervasive nature of violence against women and to confront the emotional and physical violence in our families, congregations, and communities.

Toward Safe Congregations and Right Relationship

Passed by the UUA General Assembly in 1995.
Whereas, in her report to the assembly, Executive Vice President Kay Montgomery called on our Association to promote safer congregations for women, children, and men; and

Whereas, Unitarian Universalists affirm and promote the inherent worth and dignity of every person; justice, equity, and compassion in human relations; and acceptance and encouragement to spiritual growth in our congregations; and

Because we desire Unitarian Universalist congregations to be places safe from interpersonal violence or abuse; and

Because Unitarian Universalists, along with many religious movements, have experienced incidents in which clergy or lay persons have acted in ways to jeopardize interpersonal safety within our congregations, causing pain and breach of trust; and

Because we recognize that both laity and clergy need to accept active responsibility for the prevention of interpersonal violence and abuse within our congregations and for healing where such violence or abuse has, or may occur, so that there is a restoration of community;

Whereas we recognize the moral complexity involved with the issues of justice, right relationship, power, and trust;

Therefore be it resolved that, to foster and support safe congregations and right relations, the Unitarian Universalist Association shall act, and urge its member congregations, affiliates, associates, religious professionals, and individual Unitarian Universalists to:

1. encourage education and reflection on what it means to be a safe congregation and to be persons in right relationships;
2. encourage the use of resources that examine interpersonal ethics, religious issues, and spiritual dynamics and foster safe congregations and right relations between persons;
3. utilize joint lay/clergy processes for congregational support in prevention, proactive crisis intervention, and healing, both short and long term;
4. encourage the involvement of the laity and clergy as partners in understanding issues of interpersonal ethics and in the developing of codes of conduct for laity, clergy, and congregations;
5. encourage and enhance collaboration between UUA committees and departments and affiliate/associate organizations and right relationships.

Be it further resolved that the General Assembly requests the Executive Vice President of the Unitarian Universalist Association to, for the next five years, report annually on progress in implementing this resolution.

Unitarian Universalist Association

Department of Religious Education

This department offers curricula, resources, leadership training, and religious education programs in Unitarian Universalist congregations for children, youth, and adults. The following resources are of particular significance for addressing issues of sexuality and sexual abuse.

About Your Sexuality (AYS) by deryck calderwood. (Unitarian Universalist Association, 1971, revised 1983) A comprehensive program on human sexuality, *About Your Sexuality* contains leader guides; audiovisual aids; resource books for leaders, participants, and parents; pamphlets; and games. This program helps young people to develop positive attitudes about their own sexuality and to make responsible decisions about their sexual lifestyle and behavior. *AYS* was designed to help young people get accurate information, develop their abilities to communicate with each other and with adults about sexuality, build positive and healthy attitudes and values about their own sexuality, and make responsible decisions about their sexual lifestyle and behavior.

Our Whole Lives (OWL) A Lifespan Sexuality Education Series is a joint project of the Unitarian Universalist Association and the

United Church of Christ to produce progressive, comprehensive sexuality education programs for UU congregations, UCC congregations, and secular educational settings. *OWL* will consist of five programs for five age groupings: grades K-1, grades 4-5, grades 7-9, Senior High, and Adult. While it builds on the fine foundation of *AYS*, it is a new, state-of-the-art lifespan series. All five programs will be available by 1999-2000.

About Sexual Abuse: A Program for Teens and Young Adults by Fred Ward and Betty Ward. (Unitarian Universalist Association, 1990) *About Sexual Abuse* offers exercises that help break the silence about abusive behavior. Focusing on information, prevention, and reporting, the program is organized into sections that reflect the approach taken in *About Your Sexuality*: Initiation, Interaction, Investigation, and Internalization.

ASA goals are for participants to become aware of sexual abuse; to develop an understanding of sexually abusive behaviors; to probe her or his attitudes and feelings about sexual abuse; to become more comfortable communicating feelings, values, and information about sexual abuse with others; to be alert to potentially abusive situations; to explore ways of preventing or escaping abusive situations; to learn what can be done if someone a person knows is sexually abused; to be informed about available resources in the home, church, and community for reporting sexual abuse.

In 1986 the Youth Office developed its *Code of Ethics for Persons Working with Children and Youth in Unitarian Universalist Association Sponsored Programs,* which is cited below.

The Role of Adults

Adults working with children and youth have a crucial and privileged role, one that may carry a great deal of power and influence. Whether acting as a youth advisor, chaperone, child care worker, teacher, minister, registrant at a youth-adult conference, or in other roles, an adult has a special opportunity to interact with young people in ways that are affirming and inspiring to young people and the adult. Adults can be mentors, role models, and trusted friends of children and youth. They can be teachers, counselors, and ministers. To help our children grow up to be caring and responsible adults can be a meaningful and joyful experience for the adult and a lifetime benefit to the young person.

While it is important that adults be capable of maintaining meaningful friendships with the young people they work with, adults must exercise good judgment and mature wisdom in using influence with children and young adults as well as refrain from using young people to fulfill their own needs. Young people are in a vulnerable position when dealing with adults and may find it difficult to speak out about inappropriate behavior of adults.

Adult leaders need to possess a special dedication to working with young people in ways that affirm the Unitarian Universalist

Association's Principles. Good communication skills, self awareness and understanding of others, sensitivity, problem-solving and decision-making skills, and a positive attitude are all important attributes. Additionally, in recruiting adult religious leaders we should also seek persons who have the following traits:

1. A social network outside of their religious education responsibility in which to meet their own needs for friendship, affirmation, and self-esteem.
2. Are willing and able to seek assistance from colleagues and religious professionals when they become aware of a situation requiring expert help or intervention.

It is ultimately the responsibility of the entire church or conference community, not just those in leadership positions, to create and maintain a climate that supports the growth and welfare of children and youth.

Code of Ethics for Persons Working With Children and Youth in Unitarian Universalist Association Sponsored Programs
Adults and older youth who are in leadership roles are in a position of stewardship and play a key role in fostering the spiritual development of both individuals and the community. It is therefore especially important that those in leadership positions be well qualified to provide the special nurture, care, and support that enable children and youth to develop a positive sense of self and a spirit of independence and responsibility. The relationship between young people and their leaders must be one of mutual respect if the positive potential of their relationship is to be realized.

There are no more important areas of growth than those of self-worth and the development of a healthy identity as a sexual being. Adults play a key role in assisting children and youth in these areas of growth. Wisdom dictates that children, youth, and adults suffer damaging effects when leaders become sexually involved with young people in their care: Therefore, leaders should refrain from engaging in sexual, seductive, or erotic behavior with children and youth. Neither should they sexually harass or engage in behavior with children and youth that constitutes verbal, emotional, or physical abuse.

Leaders shall be informed of this Code of Ethics and agree to it before assuming their role. In cases of violation of this code, appropriate action will be taken.

Coordinated by Patricia Hoertdoerfer, the *Safety/Abuse Clearing House packet* includes some initiatives underway in our congregations. Some of the compassionate and constructive ways Unitarian Universalists have chosen to respond include *breaking silence* through preaching and teaching, *healing services* for survivors, *support groups* for church members and community members, *education and training programs* with safety policies formulated and screening processes defined, and *prevention programs* for adults, parents, and children.

The Safety/Abuse Clearing House packet includes: a sermon by the Reverend Jade Angelica, a Unitarian Universalist minister; a healing service for survivors and congregations by the Reverend Lindi Ramsden; samples of Safety Policies and Volunteer Contract; information on reporting procedures; resource list of prevention programs; annotated bibliography of resources; and "Honoring the Children: What We Can Do to Prevent Child Abuse," a pamphlet by Patricia Hoertdoerfer and Jade Angelica

Department of Congregational, District, and Extension Services

District field staff offer consultations on congregational issues, including organizational development, leadership training, and conflict management. Extension staff work to develop congregational growth and membership diversity.

The following resources developed by this department are useful tools for understanding congregational life and dealing with sexual abuse in religious communities.

- *Congregational Handbook: How to Develop and Sustain Your Unitarian Universalist Congregation*, edited by Lawrence Peers. (Boston: UUA, 1995) Provides guidance on the advantages and responsibilities of being a member congregation of the UUA, a list of resources and services available to member congregations, and guidance on major dimensions of congregational life.
- *Mission Covenant Handbook* by John Morgan and Thomas Chulak (available from the Department of Congregational, District, and Extension Services)

District-based Safe Congregation Teams were created and trained. An example follows. In September 1994, the Mass Bay District formed a Safe Congregations Outreach Team to help Unitarian Universalist churches build safer communities by addressing issues of sexual abuse and domestic violence. The team is made up of seven Unitarian Universalists from a variety of backgrounds—some were trained by the UUA and some are professionals who work to address issues of sexual misconduct.

Using videos, experiential exercises, and discussion, the team builds congregational awareness; provides insight, knowledge, and resources; and during workshops at their church helps church members construct a preventive plan that addresses their needs.

The team conducts workshops for district meetings and annual religious educators conferences. It also talks with congregational leaders, congregations, and ministers about their experiences with sexual misconduct and boundary violations. Most districts now have Safe Congregations Outreach Teams similar to this one.

> What is a safer congregation? It is one where there has been an educational program that builds awareness and understanding of child abuse, domestic violence, clergy sexual misconduct, and sexual harassment. A safer congregation has studied the issues and appointed a representative task force.
>
> This task force, with congregational input, develops policies that help provide a safer environment. The task force also proposes action plans to deal with child abuse, sexual harassment, domestic violence, and clergy sexual misconduct. These plans include continuing education and training, avenues for reporting incidents, and documentation that the plans are being carried out regularly.
>
> For more information, contact the Safe Congregations Outreach Team, Mass Bay District Office, 110 Arlington St., Boston, MA 02116-5378. Phone (617) 542-3231; fax (617) 542-4201.

With staff members from the Departments of Ministry, Religious Education, and the executive vice president, the Department of Congregational, District, and Extension Services works as part of a clearing house team to review, communicate, and coordinate UUA staff responses to Unitarian Universalist situations and cases of sexual abuse and misconduct. This team is known as SCT-SAM (Staff Coordinating Team for Sexual Abuse and Misconduct).

Department of Ministry

By providing counsel, leadership, and resources to develop and nurture a ministry of excellence and effectiveness, the Department of Ministry serves the needs of congregations, ministers, and the Association. It develops and delivers programs ranging from credentialing and settling ministers to career counseling and ministerial congregational relations. The director of the department serves as executive secretary of the Ministerial Fellowship Committee. The Ministerial Fellowship Committee credentials ministers, sets standards for ministers, and disciplines ministers and students. It is governed by UUA bylaws and Ministerial Fellowship Committee rules and policies.

UUA-UUMA Clergy Misconduct Trainings

In 1992, ten clergy teams were trained by Marie Fortune of the Center for the Prevention of Sexual and Domestic Violence. This training was sponsored by the UUA Department of Ministry and the Unitarian Universalist Ministers Association. These teams then conducted trainings and educational workshops on clergy misconduct and sexual abuse in the ministerial relationship in most UUMA chapters, theological schools, and elsewhere as requested. Continuing education on these issues is available from the CENTER program of the UUMA.

Faith in Action

This department provides Unitarian Universalist congregations with information on social justice and racial diversity issues, prepares study guides for member congregations to vote on General Assembly Resolutions, and supplies social action training for societies, districts, and ministers.

Within Faith in Action, the Office of Bisexual, Gay, Lesbian, and Transgender Concerns developed *The Welcoming Congregation: Resources for Affirming Gay, Lesbian and Bisexual Persons*, edited by Scott Alexander (UUA, 1990). This program helps congregations become more welcoming, inclusive, and safe places for gay, lesbian, and bisexual people in their midst and in the wider community.

Department of Communications and Development

This department overseas and coordinates the publications of the Unitarian Universalist message and the development of financial support for the UUA. The *World* magazine is our denominational journal published six times a year and circulated to more than 109,000 households.

The following articles in the January/February 1993 issue of the *World* addressed the subject of clergy sexual misconduct and abuse:

- "When the Sacred Becomes Profane" by Donna Gordon, p. 20.
- "Crossing Sexual Boundaries: It Happened Here . . ." by John Lowell, p. 16.
- "Leaders Respond to Clergy Sexual Abuse" by William Schulz and others, p. 25.

Professional Organizations

Unitarian Universalist Ministers Association (UUMA)

This is the professional organization of Unitarian Universalist clergy: parish ministers, ministers of religious education, and community-based ministers. The following are statements from the UUMA Guidelines that bear on the issue of professional sexual misconduct.

UUMA Code of Professional Practices

Statement of Purpose
We, the members of the Unitarian Universalist Ministers Association, give full assent to this code of professional life as a statement of serious intent and as an expression of the lines and directions that bind us in a life of common concern, shared hopes, and firm loyalties.

1. Self

Because the religious life is a growing life, I will respect and protect my own needs for spiritual growth, ethical integrity, and continuing education to deepen and strengthen myself and my ministry.

I commit myself to honest work, believing that the honor of my profession begins with the honest use of my own mind and skills.

I will sustain a respect for the ministry. Because my private life is woven into my practice of the ministry, I will refrain from private as well as public words or actions degrading to the ministry or destructive of congregational life.

As a sexual being, I will recognize the power that ministry gives me and refrain from practices harmful to others and that endanger my integrity or professional effectiveness. Such practices include sexual activity with any child or an unwilling adult, with a counselee, with the spouse or partner of a person in the congregation, with interns, or any other exploitative relationship.

Because the demands of others upon me will be many and unceasing, I will try to be especially aware of the rights and needs of my family and my relation to them as spouse, parent, and friend.

3. Congregation

I will hold to a single standard of respect and help for all members of the church community of whatever age or position.

I will respect absolutely the confidentiality of private communications of members.

I will remember that a congregation places special trust in its professional leadership and that the members of the congregation allow a minister to become a part of their lives on the basis of that trust. I will not abuse or exploit that trust for my own gratification.

I will not invade the private and intimate bonds of others' lives, not will I trespass on those bonds for my own advantage or need when they are disturbed. In any relationship of intimate confidentiality, I will not exploit the needs of another person for my own.

I will not engage in sexual activities with a member of the congregation who is not my spouse or partner if I am married or in a committed relationship. If I am single, before becoming sexually involved with a person in the congregation, I will take special care to examine my commitment, motives, intentionality, and the nature of such activity and its consequences for myself, the other person, and the congregation.

UUA-UUMA Clergy Misconduct Trainings   See UUA Department of Ministry, p. 135, for information on CENTER Programs.

Commentary to the UU World from the UU Ministers Association

"I wonder what the ministers think about all of this?" No doubt, this is a question that was asked by many *UU World* readers in reviewing the recent articles on the subject of clergy sexual abuse.

The Unitarian Universalist Ministers Association (UUMA) welcomes the recent *World* issue devoted to the subject. The UUMA has devoted substantial and serious attention, and quite a bit of agony to this topic in recent years. It was the first of many UU organizations to do so.

Though no comment from a UUMA representative was requested by the *World*, we believe readers would be interested in knowing of our efforts and involvement in this serious issue over the last decade.

Unitarian Universalists should first understand the role of the UUMA. The Ministerial Fellowship Committee is the ministerial credentialing body for the UUA, and its responsibility is to the larger Unitarian Universalist Association, specifically, its Board of Trustees. The UU Ministers Association is the professional organization that oversees, on behalf of the ministers themselves, the professional standards of our ministry.

In 1983, the Pacific Northwest Chapter of ministers anguished over a serious situation of ministerial sexual abuse. In response, the Chapter employed the consulting help of the Reverend Marie Fortune, the foremost expert in the field, who was featured in an interview in the last issue of the *World* (Jan./Feb. 1993). As a result of its work with the Reverend Fortune, the Chapter concluded that the written ethical Code of the UUMA was inadequately vague on matters of professional sexual responsibility, and it wrote its own statement of sexual ethics, along with urging the continental UUMA to seriously study the issue.

In 1985, at the direction of the UUMA Executive Committee, a Guidelines Committee studied the issue and offered specific language that would clearly delineate in our professional Code the boundaries of clergy sexual ethics. That language, which was featured in the *World*, was adopted by the UUMA membership in 1986 and revised in 1987. Marie Fortune later commented that the UUMA statement on clergy sexual ethics was the clearest such statement of any denomination she has studied.

But we soon learned the hard lesson that simply "legislating" ethics is not enough. It was in 1989 that, as the direct result of a widely publicized case of a prominent UU minister being involved in serious predatory abusive behavior, the entire UU movement, not least of all that minister, awoke to the realization that the problem was far more widespread, and painfully, much deeper than we had imagined. Or perhaps we understood better the moral irresponsibility of silence on this issue, which had too often been the norm.

Whatever the source of the awakening, the UUMA, with the support of ministers, the UU Women's Federation, and the UUA Department of Ministry, undertook a major educational training project for ministers on the topic of clergy sexual abuse. The continuing education arm of the UUMA (CENTER) invited Marie Fortune to train teams of UU ministers, male and female, who would raise awareness and sensitivity of ministers on this issue by leading two-day workshops at each of our regional Chapter gatherings of ministers. It is the goal of the UUMA that every UU minister will experience this or a similar workshop on the subject. Over the last few years, nearly every publication of the UUMA has devoted attention to these issues. In the last year, the UUMA Executive Committee has twice taken disciplinary action against its members over violations of its sexual ethics Code…. For at least the last three years no single subject has been given more attention, either formally or in informal conversation, at ministers' gatherings than this one.

The UUMA is pleased that the Women's Federation, which has taken the lead in the larger association on this issue, has commended the Ministers Association for its work within the profession. The work is far from over, however, and the public attention to the issue inspired by the *World's* issue, which the UUMA encouraged, should help to open even wider discussion.

As UU ministers, we are disturbingly aware that each of our ministers is tarnished when any colleague violates the trust and abuses the power that is granted by the members of our congregation. The trust is a precious treasure and the UUMA is committed to protecting it by various efforts that make our professional Code mean what it says.

We believe that Unitarian Universalists deserve to know what the ministers think about all this. The UUMA is the closest we can get to expressing what UU ministers think, and with a strong and unified voice we are speaking our commitment to ethical standards that honor the trust that is placed in us.

The Executive Committee of the UUMA: the Reverend C. Leon Hopper, President, the Reverend Bets Wienecke, the Reverend Wayne Arnason, the Reverend Andrew Backus, the Reverend Bruce Clear, the Reverend Charlotte Cowtan, the Reverend Anne Heller, the Reverend Charity Rowley, the Reverend Kate Rohde

Liberal Religious Educators' Association (LREDA)

This is the professional association of religious educators, including ministers of religious education, directors of religious education, and religious education staff.

Code of
Professional
Practice

Preamble
We, the members of the Liberal Religious Educators' Association, do affirm this Code of Professional Practice as our standard of commitment to the practice of religious education. We envision and urge that this Code be followed by all LREDA members who are engaged

as professional religious educators and that it be supported by all who, in joining our membership, have indicated that they honor the importance of religious growth and learning in our congregations.

I. Self

    A. As a professional religious educator, or as a supporter of religious education, I commit myself to honor the ideals of liberal religious education and to actively explore and articulate the underlying values and principles which those ideals express.

    B. I will be faithful to those who place their trust in me. I will not abuse the power and authority of my position by manipulating others to satisfy my personal needs, which may include, but are not restricted to, sexualized behavior with: any child, adolescent, or vulnerable adult seeking advice or comfort; any adult in another committed relationship; or anyone I supervise or mentor. Nor will I engage in any other exploitative relationship that abuses the power and damages the trust that a specific individual, congregation, or institution has placed in me.

       As a religious education professional, I have the responsibility to abide by this Code of Professional Practices, and I expect that my colleagues will do likewise. I accept the responsibility to confront a colleague's misuse of power. I will call on a LREDA Good Offices representative for guidance. I will observe the legal requirements of my state or province regarding reporting of physical and sexual misconduct.

    C. Understanding that other religious education professionals will follow after me, I will actively work within an appropriately designated group within my congregation or place of employment to help establish widely recognizable, up-to-date standards of fair compensation and working conditions that support our professional skills.

    D. Because the role of and the demands on the religious educator require continual professional growth, I will seek and maintain outside collegial contacts and continuing education.

    E. As a private person who brings a complex variety of needs to my professional life, I commit myself, as much as possible, to set appropriate boundaries and to seek personal assistance outside my congregation. Although the demands of others upon me are many, I will respect my own rights and limits and those of my family.

II. Colleagues
A. Since I share the welfare of the congregation or place of employment with the parish minister and/or other staff, I will seek to be part of a mutually cooperative and consultative relationship with them as we carry out our shared and separate responsibilities. Should difficulties arise, I will seek help judiciously and express my concerns professionally, keeping in mind the dignity and value of my profession.

B. I recognize that in my relationship with colleagues in ministry, religious education, and affiliate organizations, I have a responsibility to be supportive to them and endeavor to direct them to appropriate help if necessary.

C. Understanding the trust that colleagues place in relationships with each other, I will honor the need for confidentiality, keeping in mind that such confidentiality is not to be used to allow harm to another or to prevent appropriate help from being sought.

D. I will share leadership opportunities and responsibilities with my colleagues openly, honestly, and ethically. In particular, I will consult with them in advance of any professional or public engagements that I may be asked to undertake in their communities or congregations.

E. In the event that I remain a member in the congregation where I have previously served in a position of religious education leadership, I will refrain from being involved in the process of selecting my successor. Further, I will enable my successor to establish her or his own identity and leadership in the congregation by refraining from accepting positions on policy-making bodies in the congregation (such as the board, religious education committee, finance committee, or personnel committee) for two years after my professional leadership has been concluded in that congregation. I will consult with her or him before accepting or volunteering for roles in the religious education program and will encourage members of the congregation to speak to the current religious educator of concerns.

III. Congregation
A. I will uphold and honor the practice of congregational polity within the congregation I serve, knowing that by educating and modeling the practice of such polity I am strengthening the experience of free corporate religious life.

B. I will respect the traditions of the congregation or place of employment I serve. At the same time, I am committed to seeking, in consultation with others in that body, changes that reflect liberal religious principles of inclusivity.

C. I will honor the confidences shared with me by members of the congregation or place of employment, keeping in mind that such confidentiality should not contribute to personal or professional misuse of power.

D. To achieve a well-managed transition in the case of a planned or forced resignation or significant change in role or responsibility, I will consult with a LREDA Good Offices representative or others for counsel and assistance.

IV. Wider Association
A. I will work to educate myself about and to share with others the value of the liberal religious perspective that I represent.

B. As a LREDA member, I will educate laypeople and ministerial colleagues about the dimensions of religious education leadership and will enlist their help in according appropriate status to liberal religious educators.

C. To advance professional integrity and leadership, I will know and promote LREDA's Code of Professional Practices and Guidelines.

D. I will support and participate in denominational activities and programs and encourage the participation of others in such events, knowing that this will lead to wider understanding of our goals as religious educators.

E. Recognizing the relationship between religious education values and adequate financial resources, I will work to support fair and appropriate funding efforts on behalf of my denomination and associated interests and programs.

V. The Larger Community
A. As a professional religious educator, I understand that whenever I participate in the wider community, I represent my particular faith group and should provide a model of ethical and religious leadership.

B. I will honor our liberal religious imperative to work for social justice. In turn, I will encourage people of all ages within my congregation to participate in community and world issues as the embodiment of living religiously in the liberal tradition.

LRE Journal is sponsored by LREDA and is published biannually. The fall 1994 issue theme was "Liberal Religious Responses to Violence," and the issue editor was the Reverend Lucinda Duncan.

Associate Member Organizations

The UUA Board of Trustees grants associate membership to major organizations that fulfill the following criteria: the organization's membership or constituency consists of individuals located throughout the Association and its purposes and programs are auxiliary to and supportive of the principles of the Association; the organization pledges itself to financially support the Association.

Unitarian Universalist Service Committee (UUSC)

The Unitarian Universalist Service Committee provides leadership in human rights advocacy in the United States and abroad. The UUSC's Promise the Children program works with volunteers across the country to mobilize action and education on children's issues, especially poverty, hunger, and violence.

No Punching Judy is a curriculum and video by Margi McCue, available from the UUSC. It is a five-session religious education program on the prevention of domestic violence for primary, intermediate, junior high, and senior high age groups. It also includes plans for a one-day adult workshop.

Unitarian Universalist Women's Federation (UUWF)

The Unitarian Universalist Women's Federation is the only continental membership organization for all Unitarian Universalist women. The UUWF provides programming, curriculum development, social action, support for feminist theology, and denominational leadership on many issues including antiracism and antiviolence.

In 1991 at the UUA General Assembly in Hollywood, Florida, the Board of the Unitarian Universalist Women's Federation and the UUA Women and Religion Committee issued a Call to Action to UUA and UU organizations to break the silence and to attend an open hearing on the subject of clergy sexual misconduct. As a result of this call, the Clearing House Task Force on Clergy Sexual Misconduct (Task Force I) was first convened in November 1991.

The Call to Action spoke of breaking the silence about clergy sexual misconduct and acknowledged the ongoing responses from the Department of Ministry, the Ministerial Fellowship Committee, the UU Ministers Association, the Ministerial Sisterhood, and others. The call also announced the convening of a task force, "composed of representatives from concerned UU organizations that would act as a coordinating body for the work already in progress and plan future pro-active programs of education, prevention, and healing involving both laity and clergy."

The Call to Action concluded: "We recognize that many of us would rather avoid the issue of sexual misconduct because it is a difficult issue that frightens and disturbs us. We join our voices together with concern for the victims, families, congregations, and clergy."

Meetings focused on the sharing of information about the nature and scope of the problem and the responses of the organizations represented, attempting to identify the gaps, and to suggest further actions. Twenty-eight people attended, representing the UUWF, the Women and Religion Committee, the Unitarian Universalist Association, the Society for the Larger Ministry, Unitarian Universalists Acting to Stop Violence Against Women, Starr King School for the Ministry, Unitarian Universalist Ministers Association, Ministerial Sisterhood UU, Liberal Religious Educators' Association, and the Mass Bay Ethics Group. Representatives of Meadville/Lombard Theological School, Collegium, Ferry Beach, and the UUA Task Force attended later meetings.

The following are useful resources:

- Mary Moore, with Betty Hoskins, Mairi Maeks, Phyllis Rickter, *Finding Our Way: Responding to Clergy Sexual Misconduct* (Boston, MA: The Unitarian Universalist Women's Federation, 1992). Poses theological and institutional questions evoked by clergy sexual misconduct and reviews responses of 38 other denominations.
- Carolyn Nickel, "Soul Murder: The Horrific Abuse of Children," UUWF *Communicator*, March/April 1991
- Judi Doherty, "M-I-S-O-G-Y-N-Y," UUWF *Communicator*, May/June 1991
- Metro Men Against Violence, Toronto, ONT, "A Man's Pledge to Work to End Men's Violence," UUWF *Communicator*, May/June 1991
- Phyllis Rickter, "Task Force on Clergy Sexual Misconduct," UUWF *Communicator*, January/February 1992
- Hala Dub Jabbour, "A Trail of Tragedies," from *Update Newsletter* of Religions Network for Equality for Women, January/February 1992
- Frances Park, "Enabling or Breaking the Silence: Parishioners' Role in Ministerial Sexual Misconduct," UUWF *Communicator*, March/April 1992

- Reviews of Collegium publication "Feminist Thought on Sexual Ethics" and UUWF member publication "Domestic Violence, A Reference Handbook," UUWF *Communicator*, November/December 1993
- Alison Cooper, "Domestic Violence: A Primer for UUs," UUWF *Communicator*, September/October 1994
- Phyllis Rickter, "UU Task Force on Sexual Abuse and Clergy Misconduct . . . The Goal Is Safe, Nurturing Congregations for All UUs," UUWF *Communicator*, November/December 1994
- "Eve and Mary" [pseudonyms],"Young UU Women Speak: Yes, This Happened to Us, UUWF *Communicator*, June/July 1995
- Bill Sinkford, "Safety As a Spiritual Gift," UUWF *Communicator*, June/July 1995
- Jory Agate, "A Response of Concern," UUWF *Communicator*, June/July 1995
- Cindy Spring and Rob Cavenaugh, letters, UUWF *Communicator*, June/July 1995.

Vision Statement and Call to UUA Board
Task Force I on Clergy Sexual Misconduct
October 1994

To UUA Board of Trustees:

We, the members of Task Force I on Clergy Sexual Misconduct, after meeting for the past two years, believe that it is our challenge as a religious association of congregations to see that our societies are safe places for all people: women, children, and men, clergy and laity.

We are pleased that work has been done to deal with reported incidents of clergy misconduct. However, the work done by the Task Force on Congregational Response to Ministerial Sexual Misconduct is only a beginning.

To build nurturing and supportive religious communities, our societies need to be places where people of all ages can be free from the threat of physical, psychological, and sexual abuse and/or harassment. Our vision of safe societies must be expanded to ensure that all Unitarian Universalists have the freedom to grow responsibly in spirit and without fear.

We reach out to you, the trustees of our Association, because we need to know that our concerns are your concerns. We hope to see the UUA continue to fund and take constructive action to ensure that our societies are safe havens for religious growth for all who are associated with us. We believe it is the moral thing to do. Also, in light of increased litigation against religious institutions, we believe prevention of abusive behavior is prudent.

As representatives of UUA staff, and UU affiliate and associate organizations meeting as a coordinating body, we ask the UUA Board of Trustees to affirm its responsibility to ensure that the Association foster safe places to worship and to join in fellowship, and that the

Board agree to meet with us at its earliest convenience to discuss strategies to ensure safety in our societies. We urge that you support our call to compassion and justice.

Members of Task Force I on Clergy Sexual Misconduct represent the following departments of the UUA and the following organizations: Department of Ministry, Department of Religious Education, UU Ministers Association, Liberal Religious Educators' Association, UU Women's Federation, Continental Women and Religion Committee, MSUU: Ministerial Sisterhood, Society for the Larger Ministry, Collegium, Unitarian Universalists Acting to Stop Violence Against Women, Starr King School for the Ministry, and Meadville/Lombard Theological School.

Independent Affiliate Organization

The UUA Board of Trustees grants independent affiliate status to independently constituted and operated organizations whose purposes and intentions are found to be in sympathy with the principles of the Association, and who support the Association by paying an annual contribution.

UUs Acting to Stop Violence Against Women

UUs Acting to Stop Violence Against Women provides educational programs, resources, and networking with concerned Unitarian Universalists.

Theological School

Meadville/Lombard Midwinter Institutes

The 1993 Institute for Religious Professionals focused on sexual abuse, including clergy misconduct and child abuse, with speaker the Reverend Marie Fortune from the Center for the Prevention of Sexual and Domestic Violence.

The theme for the 1996 Institute was "Turning Back the Tide of Violence" with Geoffrey Canada and Thandeka as presenters and facilitators.

Forum

Collegium: An Association for Liberal Religious Studies

A good resource to read is *Edge of the Wave: Feminist Thought on Sexual Ethics,* edited by Susann Pangerl (Chicago, IL: Collegium, 1993)

Bibliography

Clergy Misconduct and Abuse

Barnhouse, Ruth Tiffany. *Clergy and the Sexual Revolution*. Bethesda, MD: Alban Institute, 1987.

Fortune, Marie. "Confidentiality and Mandatory Reporting: A False Dilemma?" Chicago: Christian Century Foundation, *The Christian Century*, June 18-25, 1986.

_____. *Is Nothing Sacred? When Sex Invades the Pastoral Relationship*. San Francisco: Harper and Row, 1989.

_____ *Training Manual on Clergy Misconduct: Sexual Abuse in Ministerial Relationships*. Seattle, WA: Center for Prevention of Sexual Domestic Violence, 1992

Hopkins, Nancy M. *Clergy Sexual Misconduct: A Systems Approach*. Bethesda, MD: Alban Institute, 1993.

_____. *The Congregation Is Also a Victim: Sexual Abuse and the Violation of Pastoral Trust*. Bethesda, MD: Alban Institute, 1992.

Laasar, Mark and Nancy Hopkins. *Healing the Soul of a Church: Congregations Wounded by Clergy Sexual Misconduct*. Bethesda, MD: Alban Institute, 1995.

Lebacqz, Karen and Ronald Barton. *Sex in the Parish*. Louisville, KY: Westminster/John Knox Press, 1991.

Knudsen, Chilton R. "Trauma Debriefing: A Congregational Model." *Conciliation Quarterly*, Volume 10, No. 2, Spring 1991.

Parrot, Andrea. "Acquaintance Rape and Sexual Assault Prevention," in *Sexual Assault and Abuse: A Handbook for Clergy and Religious Professionals*. Edited by Barbara Chester and Jane Boyajian. New York: Harper and Row, 1987.

Peterson, Marilyn R. *At Personal Risk: Boundary Violations in Professional-Client Relationships*. New York: W.W. Norton, 1992.

Rediger, G. Lloyd. *Ministry and Sexuality: Cases, Counseling and Care.* Minneapolis: Fortress Press, 1990.

Rutter, Peter. *Sex in the Forbidden Zone.* Los Angeles: Jeremy Tarcher, 1989.

Tracey, Denise. *Healing the Congregation.* Bethesda, MD: Alban Institute, 1995.

Clergy Self-Care

Hands, Donald and Wayne Fehr. *Spiritual Wholeness for Clergy: A New Psychology of Intimacy with God, Self and Others.* Bethesda, MD: Alban Institute, 1993.

Harbaugh, Gary. *Caring for the Caregiver: Growth Models for Professional Leaders and Congregations.* Bethesda, MD: Alban Institute, 1993.

Oswald, Roy. *Clergy Self-Care: Finding a Balance for Effective Ministry,* Bethesda, MD: Alban Institute, 1991.

Sexual Harassment and Abuse

Adams, Caren and Jennifer Fay. *Nobody Told Me It Was Rape.* Santa Cruz, CA: Network Publications, 1984.

Bass, Ellen and Laura Davis. *The Courage to Heal: A Guide for Women Survivors of Child Sexual Abuse.* New York: HarperCollins, 1988.

Bell, Linda. *Rethinking Ethics in the Midst of Violence: A Feminist Approach to Freedom.* Lanham, MD: Rowan and Littlefield, 1993.

Blume, E. Sue. *Secret Survivors: Uncovering Incest and Its Aftereffects in Women.* New York: Ballantine Books, 1990.

Burson, Malcolm. "Broken Silence, Mending Lives: One Parish's Response to Family Violence and Sexual Abuse." *Action Information,* Nov./Dec. 1987. Bethesda, MD: Alban Institute.

Carnes, Patrick. *Out of the Shadows: Understanding Sexual Addition.* Minneapolis: CompCare, 1992.

Clark, Donald. *Sexual Abuse in the Church: The Law Steps In.* Chicago: *The Christian Century,* 1993.

Davis, Laura. *Allies in Healing.* New York: Harper Perennial, 1991.

_____. *The Courage to Heal Workbook: For Men and Women Survivors of Child Sexual Abuse.* New York: HarperCollins Publishers, Inc., 1990.

_____. *The Courage to Heal Workbook: A Guide for Women Survivors of Child Sexual Abuse.* New York: HarperCollins Publishers, Inc., 1990.

Enroth, Ronald. *Recovering from Churches that Abuse.* Grand Rapids, MI: Zondervan, 1994.

Fay, Jennifer J. and Billie Jo Flerchinger. *Top Secret: Sexual Assault Information for Teenagers Only (2nd ed.).* Renton, WA: King County Rape Relief, 1988.

Fortune, Marie. *Keeping the Faith: Questions and Answers for the Abused Woman.* San Francisco: Harper, 1987.

_____. *Love Does No Harm: Sexual Ethics for the Rest of Us.* New York: Continuum, 1995.

_____. *Sexual Violence: The Unmentionable Sin.* New York: Pilgrim Press, 1983.

Frederickson, Renee. *Repressed Memories: A Journey to Recovery from Sexual Abuse.* New York: Simon and Schuster, 1992.

Gil, Eliana. *Outgrowing the Pain Together: A Book for Spouses and Partners of Adults Abused as Children.* New York: Dell, 1992.

Groth, A. Nicholas. *Men Who Rape: The Psychology of the Offender.* New York: Plenum, 1979.

Hahn, Celia. *Sexual Paradox: Creative Tensions in Our Lives and in Our Congregations.* New York: Pilgrim, 1991.

Herman, Judith Lewis. *Trauma and Recovery: The Aftermath of Violence—From Domestic Abuse to Political Terror.* New York: Basic Books, 1992.

Hindman, Jan. *Step by Step: Sixteen Steps Toward Legally Sound Sexual Abuse Investigation.* Ontario, OR: AlexAndria Associates, 1987. (911 SW Third St., Ontario, OR, 97914)

Hoskins, Betty. "Comforting the Bystanders and Cleansing the Religious Community." *Edge of the Wave: Feminist Thought on Sexual Ethics.* Edited by Susann Pangerl. Collegium Occasional Papers No. 3. (5701 S. Woodlawn Ave., Chicago, IL 60637)

Hunt, Mary. *Fierce Tenderness: A Feminist Theology of Friendship.* New York: Crossroad, 1992.

Jinkins, Michael and Deborah Jinkins. *Power and Change in Parish Ministry: Reflections on the Cure of Souls.* Bethesda, MD: Alban Institute, 1991.

Kegan, Robert. *In Over Our Heads: The Mental Demands of Modern Life.* Cambridge, MA: Harvard University Press, 1994.

Lew, Mike. *Victims No Longer: Men Recovering from Incest and Other Sexual Child Abuse.* New York: Nevraumont, 1988.

McNeal, John, et al. *Sexual Ethics and the Church: A Christian Century Symposium.* Chicago, IL: Christian Century Magazine, 1989.

Miller, Sherod, Daniel B. Wackman, Elam W. Nunnally, and Carol Saline. *Straight Talk: A New Way to Get Close to Others by Saying What You Really Mean.* New York: New American Library, 1982.

Moore, Mary, et al. *Finding Our Way: Responding to Clergy Sexual Misconduct.* Volume III in the *Transforming Thought Series,* A Unitarian Universalist Women's Federation Report to the Unitarian Universalist Task Force on Clergy Sexual Misconduct, 1992. Boston, MA: UUWF, 25 Beacon St., Boston, MA 02108.

Parker, Rebecca. "Making Love As a Means of Grace." *1992 Selected Essays, Unitarian Universalist Ministers Association.* Edited by Thomas Wintle. Boston: Unitarian Universalist Ministers Association, 1992.

Parrot, Andrea. *Coping with Date Rape and Acquaintance Rape.* New York: Rosen Publishing, 1988.

Pellauer, Mary, et al., eds. *Sexual Assault and Abuse: A Handbook for Clergy and Religious Professionals.* New York: Harper and Row, 1987.

Russell, Diana E.H. *Sexual Exploitation: Rape, Child Sexual Abuse and Workplace Harassment.* Beverly Hills, CA: Sage, 1986.

Star, Barbara. *Helping the Abuser: Intervening Effectively in Family Violence.* New York: Family Service Association of America, 1983.

Taylor, Cathryn L. *The Inner Child Workbook: What to Do With Your Past When It Just Won't Go Away.* New York: Putnam's, 1991.

Viscott, David. *The Language of Feelings.* New York: Pocket Books, 1976.

Warshaw, Robin. *I Never Called It Rape: The Ms. Report on Recognizing, Fighting, and Surviving Date and Acquaintance Rape.* New York: Harper and Row, 1988.

Whitfield, Charles. *Boundaries and Relationships: Knowing, Protecting and Enjoying the Self.* Deerfield Beach, FL: Health Communications, 1993.

_____. *Healing the Child Within.* Deerfield Beach, FL: Health Communications, 1987.

Woititz, Janet G. *Healing Your Sexual Self.* Deerfield Beach, FL: Health Communications Inc., 1989.

Child Abuse and Neglect

Adams, Caren. "Considering Children's Developmental Stages in Prevention Education," in Mary Nelson and Kay Clark, ed., *The Educator's Guide to Preventing Child Sexual Abuse.* Santa Cruz, CA: Network Publications, 1981.

Angelica, Jade C. *A Moral Emergency: Breaking the Cycle of Child Sexual Abuse.* Kansas City, MO: Sheed & Ward, 1993.

_____. *We Are Not Alone . . . : A Teenage Girl's Personal Account of Incest from Disclosure through Prosecution and Treatment.* Somerville, MA: Justice for Children, Inc., 1992. (Office of the District Attorney, Middlesex County, 21 McGrath Highway, Somerville, MA 02143.)

Arnason, Wayne, et al. *L.I.F.T.: Life Issues for Teenagers*. Boston: Unitarian Universalist Association, 1985.

Berrick, Jill Duerr and Neil Gilbert. *With the Best of Intentions: The Child Sexual Abuse Prevention Movement*. New York: The Guilford Press, 1991.

Bolton, Frank G., Jr., Larry P. Morris and Ann E. MacEachron. *Males at Risk: The Other Side of Child Sexual Abuse*. Newbury Park, CA: Sage, 1989.

Briere, John N. *Child Abuse Trauma: Theory and Treatment of the Lasting Effects*. Newbury Park, CA: Sage Publications, Inc. 1992.

Bulkley, Josephine, et al. *Dealing with Sexual Child Abuse*. Chicago: National Committee for the Prevention of Child Abuse, 1982.

Burgess, Ann. *The Sexual Victimization of Adolescents*. Rockville, MD: National Institute of Mental Health, 1985.

Burgess, Ann W., et al. *Sexual Assault of Children and Adolescents*. Lexington, MA: Lexington Books, 1978.

calderwood, deryck. *About Your Sexuality (2nd ed.)*. Boston, MA: Unitarian Universalist Association, 1983.

Carlson, Lee W. *Child Sexual Abuse: A Handbook for Clergy and Church Members*. Valley Forge, PA: Judson, 1988.

Colao, Flora and Tamar Hosansky. *Your Children Should Know: Personal Safety Strategies for Parents to Teach Their Children*. New York: Harper and Row, 1987.

Elliott, Michele, ed. *Female Sexual Abuse of Children*. New York: Guilford Press, 1993.

Finkelhor, David. *Child Sexual Abuse: New Theory and Research*. New York: Free Press, 1984.

_____. "The Prevention of Child Sexual Abuse: An Overview of Needs and Problems." New York: Sex Information and Education Council of the U.S., SIECUS Report, Vol. XIII, No. 1, September 1984.

_____. *A Sourcebook on Child Sexual Abuse*. Newbury Park, CA: Sage, 1986.

Flerchinger, Billie Jo and Jennifer J. Fay. *Top Secret: A Discussion Guide*. Santa Cruz, CA: Network, 1985.

Fortune, Marie. *Sexual Abuse Prevention: A Study for Teenagers*. New York: United Church Press, 1984.

Fraser, Brian G. *The Educator and Child Abuse*. Chicago, IL: National Committee for the Prevention of Child Abuse, 1981.

Freeman, Lory. *It's My Body*. Seattle, WA: Parenting Press, Inc., 1983. [Parents guide and companion book—*Protect Your Child From Sexual Assault* by Janie Hart-Ross. Seattle, WA: Parenting Press, 1984.]

Greven, Philip. *Spare the Child: The Religious Roots of Punishment and the Psychological Impact of Physical Abuse*. New York: Vintage Books, 1990.

Hammar, Richard R., Steven W. Klipowicz, and James F. Cobble, Jr. *Reducing the Risk of Child Sexual Abuse in Your Church Program*. Matthews, NC: Church Law and Tax Report, Christian Ministry Resources, 1993. (resource book, training manual, and video)

Haugaard, Jeffrey J. and N. Dickon Reppucci. *The Sexual Abuse of Children: A Comprehensive Guide to Current Knowledge and Intervention Strategies*. San Francisco, CA: Jossey-Bass, 1988.

Hindman, Jan. *Abuse to Sexual Abuse Prevention Programs—or—Ways We Abuse Our Children as We Attempt to Prevent Abuse*. Ontario, OR: AlexAndria Associates, 1984. (AlexAndria Associates, 911 SW Third St., Ontario, OR 97914)

_____. *A Very Touching Book . . . For Little People and for Big People . . .* Durkee, OR: McClure-Hindman Associates, 1984.

Mather, Cynthia, with Kristina E. Doebye. *How Long Does It Hurt? A Guide to Recovering from Incest and Sexual Abuse for Teenagers, Their Friends, and Their Families*. San Francisco: Jossey-Bass, 1994.

Miller, Alice. *For Your Own Good: Hidden Cruelty in Child-rearing and the Roots of Violence*. New York: Farrar-Straus-Giroux, 1983.

_____. *Thou Shalt Not Be Aware: Society's Betrayal of the Child*. New York: New American Library, 1984.

Nelson, Mary and Kay Clark. *The Educator's Guide to Preventing Child Sexual Assault*. Santa Cruz, CA: Network Publications of ETR Associates, 1987.

Plummer, Carol A. *Preventing Sexual Abuse: Activities and Strategies for Those Working with Children and Adolescents*. Holes Beach, FL: Learning Publications, 1984.

Sanford, Linda R. *Come Tell Me Right Away*. Rayethville, NY: EdUPress, Inc., 1982.

_____. *The Silent Children: A Parent's Guide to the Prevention of Child Sexual Abuse*. New York: McGraw-Hill, 1982.

Scott, Jeffrey Warren. "Confidentiality and Child Abuse: Church and State Collide." *The Christian Century*, February 19, 1986, Christian Century Foundation.

Soukup, Ruth, Sharon Wickner, and Joanne Corbette. *Three in Every Classroom: The Child Victim of Incest—What You as a Teacher Can Do*.

Gonvick, MN: Richards Publishing, 1984.

Tower, Cynthia Crosson. *Child Abuse and Neglect: A Teacher's Handbook for Detection Reporting and Classroom Management.* Washington, DC: National Educational Association, 1984.

_____. *How Schools Can Help Combat Child Abuse and Neglect (2nd ed.).* Washington, DC: National Education Association, 1987.

Ward, Fred and Betty Ward. *About Sexual Abuse: A Program for Teens and Young Adults.* Boston: Unitarian Universalist Association, 1990.

Wexler, Richard. *Wounded Innocents: The Real Victims of the War Against Child Abuse.* Buffalo, NY: Prometheus Books, 1995.

Other Resources

Chulak, Tom and John Morgan. *Growing: A Congregational Enhancement Series for Unitarian Universalists.* Boston: Unitarian Universalist Association, 1987.

Journal of Interpersonal Violence. Newbury Park, CA: Sage.

Peers, Larry, ed. *UUA Congregational Handbook.* Boston: Unitarian Universalist Association, 1995.

Psychotherapy Letter. Providence, RI: Manisses Communications Group.

SIECUS Journal. New York: Sex Information and Education Council of the United States.

Working Together to Prevent Sexual and Domestic Violence. Seattle, WA: Center for the Prevention of Sexual and Domestic Violence.

Audiovisual Resources

Better Safe Than Sorry II. 16 mm or video, 15 minutes. Filmfair Communications, 1983. (10900 Ventura Boulevard, PO Box 1728, Studio City, CA 91605; (818) 985-0244). Video available through the UUA Video Loan Library.

No More Secrets. 16 mm or video, 13 minutes. ODN Publications, 1982. 74 Varick St., Suite 304, New York, NY 10013; (212) 431-8923.

No Easy Answers. Video, 32 minutes. Illusion Theater, 1987. Available through the UUA Video Loan Library.

An Ounce of Prevention. Three 18-minute videos for three age groups: 4-8, 9-11, and 12-14. Agency for Instructional Technology, 1983 (Box A, Bloomington, IN 47402, (800) 458-4509 or (800) 339-2203). (These videos will be distributed under another title. Contact AIT for information.)

Touch. 16 mm or video, 32 minutes. MTI Teleprograms, 1984. (3710 Commercial Avenue, Northbrook, IL 60062, (800) 323-6031) 16 mm film available through the UUA Video Loan Library.

From the Center for Prevention of Sexual and Domestic Violence, 1914 North 34th Street, Suite 105, Seattle, WA 98103, (206) 634-1903:

Bless Our Children: Preventing Sexual Abuse, 1993, video, 40 minutes.

Broken Vows: Religious Perspectives on Domestic Violence. 1994, two-part video—Part I is 37 minutes, Part II is 22 minutes.

Hear Their Cries: Religious Response to Child Abuse, 1992, video, 48 minutes.

Not in My Church. 1991, video, 45 minutes.

Contributors

Since 1993, **Nancy Bowen** has served as District Executive of the Central Massachusetts and Connecticut Valley Districts. She is a community minister and before working as a District Executive she was struggling to develop congregation-based social justice programs. A birthright Unitarian Universalist, Nancy earned an MDiv. from Yale Divinity School and a BA from Smith College.

Patricia Hoertdoerfer is the Children's Program Director of the UUA Department of Religious Education. As a religious educator for more than 20 years and a minister of religious education, Pat has served churches in Syracuse, NY, and Bethesda, MD. She was trained by Marie Fortune as a workshop leader on issues of clergy misconduct. She also coordinates the *Safety/Abuse Clearing House packet* for the Department of Religious Education.

Betty B. Hoskins was the founding chair of the Feminist Theology Awards of the Unitarian Universalist Women's Federation. She has chaired Collegium, the association of liberal religious scholars, and is a member of Task Force I. An active laywoman, she has been author and editor of numerous articles and monographs about biology, bioethics, feminist thought, acting against violence, and teaching. Betty is an Associate Professor of Sciences at the Massachusetts College of Art and a freelance editor for science textbooks and monographs. She is a life member of the UUWF and has been a member of congregations in Baltimore, MD, Amherst, MA, Dallas, TX, and Grafton-Upton, MA.

A member of the Unitarian Universalist Church at Washington Crossing in Titusville, NJ, for 12 years, **Michelle Hunt** has worked on a variety of standing and ad hoc committees, served as a trustee, and served two terms as president of the board. During her term as president, the congregation learned of allegations of sexual misconduct by a former minister. Because of her background as a lay leader in a congregation with this type of experience, Michelle was invited to serve on the UUA Task Force on Congregational Response to Clergy Sexual Misconduct.

 **Fredric John Muir** is parish minister of the Annapolis Unitarian Universalist Church in Maryland. A graduate of Union Theological Seminary in New York, he received his DMin. from Wesley Theological Seminary in Washington, DC. He was trained by Marie Fortune as a workshop leader on the issue of clergy misconduct. He is also the author of *A Reason For Hope: Liberation Theology Confronts a Liberal Faith* (Carmel, CA: Sunflower Ink, 1994).

 **Deborah J. Pope-Lance** is a licensed therapist and a minister in fellowship with the Unitarian Universalist Association. She has served as a parish minister in New Jersey and Massachusetts. As a community minister, she is currently in private practice in Boston and Sudbury, MA, providing individual and couples therapy and teaching and consulting on the ethics of ministerial practice.

 **Phyllis Rickter** has been a member of the Arlington Street Church of Boston, MA, since 1965. She served on the Administrative Board of the Unitarian Universalist Women's Federation for 12 years, including four years as continental president.

 **William Sinkford** is the Director of the UUA Department for Congregational, District, and Extension Services. He earned a BA from Harvard College in 1968 and an MDiv. from Starr King School for the Ministry in 1994. He convenes the UUA's Staff Coordinating Team for Sexual Abuse and Misconduct.

 **Gretchen Thomas** served as Associate Minister responsible for religious education at the First Unitarian Church of San Jose, CA, before moving to Toronto, ONT, in 1991. She is currently the Campus Chaplain for Unitarian Universalist students, staff, and faculty at the University of Toronto. Gretchen is a board member of the Church of the Larger Fellowship and is very active in the Transylvania/Czech Partner Church Movement.

Acknowlegments continued from copyright page.

"Benediction" by Susan Manker-Seale is from *Awakened From the Forest* (Boston: Skinner House Books). Copyright © 1995 by the Unitarian Universalist Association. Reprinted by permission.

A Healthy Religious Education Community
Opening words are by the Reverend Donna DiSciullo, Director of Young Adult Ministries, Unitarian Universalist Association. Reprinted by permission of the author.

"Home for the Spirit of the Child" is by the Reverend Judith Meyer, Unitarian Community Church, Santa Monica, CA. Reprinted by permission of the author.

Closing words are by the Reverend John Cummins, Minneapolis, MN. Reprinted by permission of the author.

Teacher dedication is by Elizabeth Motander Jones, Director of Religious Education, First Unitarian Universalist Church, San Diego, CA. Reprinted by permission of the author.

"Non-Violence and Unitarian Universalist Principles" in the discussion essay is by the Reverend Colleen McDonald, The Unitarian Universalist Church, Rockford, IL. It is adapted from "Violent Free Zone" by the Loretto Community's SAVE Campaign, St. Louis, MO. Used by permission.

The Courage to Heal
Opening and closing words are from "Re-Weaving the Threads, A Movement Toward Wholeness" by the Reverend Donna DiSciullo, Director of Young Adult Ministries, Unitarian Universalist Association. Reprinted by permission of the author.

"Forgiveness" is by Sara Moores Campbell. Reprinted by permission of the author.

The diagram of dimensions of congregational healing is from "Trauma Debriefing: A Congregational Model" by Chilton R. Knudsen in *Conciliation Quarterly* (Mennonite), Vol. 10, No. 2, Spring 1991. Copyright © 1991 by Chilton R. Knudsen. Reprinted by permission of the author.

Excerpts from *The Courage to Heal: A Comprehensive Guide to Healing from Child Sexual Abuse* in the discussion essay are by Ellen Bass and Laura Davis (New York, NY: HarperPerennial). Copyright © 1994 by HarperPerennial (a division of HarperCollins Publishers, Inc.).

Creating and Reviewing Our Covenant
Congregational mission and covenant statements are from the Dublin Unitarian Universalist Church, Powell, OH, and the Unitarian Universalist Church, Corpus Christi, TX. Reprinted by permission.